WORD-TEMPLE PERSON

Also by Ann Keiffer

Gift of the Dark Angel:
A Woman's Journey Through
Depression Towards Wholeness

Somebody's Life
(poems)

WORD-TEMPLE PERSON

poems

by
Ann L. Keiffer

ShadowDance Press

© 2007 by Ann Keiffer. All rights reserved.
ShadowDance Press

ISBN: 978-0-6151-4207-4

Cover photograph copyright © 2007
Whitney A. Brandt
You can find more photography by Whitney at
www.uglygreenchair.com

Before You Begin...

Whence cometh this title: *Word-Temple Person*?
In the elegant and beautiful brush-stroke kanji
characters of Asia, the literal translation of the
kanji for POET is WORD-TEMPLE PERSON.

With love and gratitude I dedicate *Word-Temple
Person* to Dr. Clare Morris, Rev. Kristi Denham,
and my husband Larry. Each of you in your own
way supports the soulwork that is the center
and Source of my life…and all my poems.

CONTENTS

First-Time Grammy

Snow-Globe	2
Dancing Miss Daisy	4
Rocking Chair's Got Me	6
Daisy Stands Straight Up	8
Daisy's Big, Wide World	10
My Inheritance I Give You	13
Daisy in the Garden	15
Grace	17
Daisy, Not Napping	18
The Lion-Shaman	20
Mammories	22

Daily Lessons

Singing Christmas	24
Bill Gates Doesn't Love Words	26
Impersonating Elvis	28
Too Much in the World	32
Bad Week	33
Ugly Dog	34
What If?	35
Fetch Me a Lick of Sense	38
Crash Course	41
She'd Rather I Were Lying	46

The State of Things

War Poem for a Little Girl in a White Dress	50
Heads-of-State Grudge Match	52
Being Seen	54
Of Hawks and Doves	57
Driving by a Bus Stop	60
The Devil Takes All	62
Suicide Bombers	67
The Zen of Ants	74
What To Do After You've Seen the Wizard	76
Broken Things	79
I Want To Turn Away	82
Consumed by Consumption	84

Little Redeemer Child   86

Beloveds
Retiring Early   88
Hard-Hatted Woman with Band-Aids   90
The 5-Minute Kiss   92
Crying Over Enchiladas   94
My Racy Corvette   97
Spicy Mama   99
Don't Take This Away from Me   103
Bird with a Broken Wing   105
Warms His Hands, Too   107
On Not Saying   109

Intimate Mysteries
Green Mother   114
My Pearl of Great Price   117
Seeing God for the First Time   119
Speaking in Tongues of Prayer   120
God's Eyes   124
Windsocks   127
Available   129
Getting the Message   132
Teeter-Totter   133
The Zero in the O of NO   136

Life, Death & In-Between
Vines   138
Humble Pie   142
The Eyes of Death Are Deep   144
Watchers   147
Yes-M'am   153
Birthing Her Mother   156
Not Too Distressed   159
Call in the Crows   161
We Can See It from Here   165
What You Left   166
The Last Time   173
The Golden Chord   175
Charade   176

First-Time Grammy

Snow Globe

For me, being a new grandmother
is like looking in on a snow globe
and discovering
an enchanted world
I have never known before:
Sweet Grandbaby Land.
To my grammy-eyes
the snow falling in this snow globe
isn't even pretending to be snow.
In the weeks just after
our only grandchild's birth,
what I see floating down
on my son's new little family
are tiny, iridescent crystals
of unimagined magic.

The magic floats gently down
on the father changing a diaper,
on the mother putting her baby to her breast,
on an infant learning to make
her new-baby needs known
in the inchoate language of crying,

Do they know how beautiful they are?
I know they have dark circles
under their eyes from lack of sleep.
I know my son's 5:00 shadow
has a date-and-time stamp
that expired yesterday or before.
I know their clothes are
a bit rumpled,
their hair a bit rumpled,
the house a bit rumpled,
and the wee, scrawny babe
so fragile you can nearly
see through her skin.
And yet, they are almost
too beautiful to look upon,

like seeing God
and being struck blind.

I was a new mother once.
But how different this is.
I wasn't holding the snow-globe
at a generation's distance then,
wasn't on the outside looking in,
wasn't old enough to feel
the presence of this little child
as both a kind of completion
and a lifetime of beginnings.
The intimate circle of family
opens to take this child in,
surrounding and embracing her
in the family's sphere of love.
The forecast is permanent:
A possibility of flurries
of iridescent miracles.
Though sometimes
this may include
a little shaking up.

For my son, John

Dancing Miss Daisy

For three-month-old Daisy
it was a cranky-pants day,
sleeping for fifteen minutes
or half-an-hour at a time,
waking herself up
just to make sure
she wasn't missing anything,
then laughing, crying, screaming
all at the same time,
too tired to give in
to the quiet, boring passivity of sleep.

Grammy and Papa are visiting,
and we watch as our son,
the new stay-at-home Dad,
walks Daisy all around the house,
holding her in that new-fangled,
facing-out, more-social-baby way.
And Daisy sits in the crook
of her Daddy's elbow,
her arm resting along his,
like she's the Queen
surveying her queendom:
LuLee, the dog;
the front yard;
Papa watching Queen Daisy
most adoringly from the couch;
Grammy cooking in the kitchen;
the photographs on the mantel…
oops, there for a minute
Daisy almost forgot she was crabby,
but now she starts cranking up again.

So what does Daddy do?
He gets the Snugli baby-carrier,
straps his darling daughter on his chest,

facing outward, of course.
And he puts on the CD player
the loudest, most git-down,
boogie-your-socks-off music ever.
And he starts dancing Daisy
all around the living room.
He's wild, he's crazy, a twist,
a thrust, a turn, a leap,
a backward-forward step
for every hit of the beat.
And all the while Daisy sits securely
in her baby-carrier on his chest,
only her little arms and legs loose…
and flopping about all relaxed,
like a rag dolly dancing girl.

The beat goes on and so does Daddy,
running through every kick, spin,
turn, shake, and hip-flick performed
on the hippest dance floor.
And Daisy's not crying anymore.
And Daddy is smiling.
No, Daddy is laughing!
He's getting the hang
of this parenting thing
in the way that Daddies do best:
He's playing.

And Grammy, too, is laughing,
seeing the living, leaping,
proof that my son's
sometime cycles of depression
and its cruel twin, self-loathing,
just might be
losing their grip on him.
Today he is laughing, joyous, expressive,
creative and funny-crazy, dancing Daisy.

Could it be that Daisy
is dancing Daddy, too?

Rocking Chair's Got Me

Today I sat in the rocking chair,
my baby grand-daughter Daisy,
who never wants to close her eyes,
finally asleep on my shoulder.
She had cried on her blanket
on the floor, in her crib,
in her swing, in my arms...
until all I could do was
hold her to me and rock her,
whisper-singing
shhhhhh in her ear,
followed by every song I ever knew,
until she finally conked out,
one tear still stuck on her cheek.

In the quiet of the afternoon,
as Daisy and I sat and rocked,
the sun reached its shining arms
in through the shutters and
threw down a golden veil round us.
The first scents of spring
sidled in the open door,
took a spin around the room,
and winked at us.

There was no hurry or scurry in me,
All that mattered was rocking Daisy,
...listening to her baby-snore,
...grinning to myself
as her lips twitched in sleep
to smile or pout or phantom-suck,
...noticing how the weave-pattern
of my cotton sweater
was imprinting on her cheek,
Daisy's sweet, soft body
draped warmly across my belly,
my breast, my chest, my shoulder--
my cheek against her head.

just rocking Daisy
and watching her sleep.

As the clock tick-tocked and I rocked,
everything in me was
soft-singing with happiness.
And an amazing thought came:
Even though I have crested
the hill of middle-age
and am heading into old at quite a clip,
some parts of me are still being born.

I didn't know I had
this Grandmother-self in me,
this contented, adoring, slowed down,
no-need-to-get-out-of-the-chair,
relaxed, bystander, on-looker Grammy.
Perhaps there are other selves and
more to learn about living into old age
than we have been led to believe.
Big thought. Time will tell.
Anyway,
the old rocking chair's
already got me now.
And I'm sitting in it,
just rocking Daisy.

Daisy Stands Straight Up

My daughter-in-law calls me,
reporting excitedly,
"There Daisy was, just sitting
in the middle of the floor,
eating paper,
when she stood straight up!"

Eating paper?
That makes me laugh.
But Daisy stood up?
That spins my head around!
My grand-daughter Daisy
just stood right up.
One minute she couldn't,
and the next minute
that's exactly what she did.

A few days later
when I am with Daisy,
I watch her crawling,
pulling herself up
to the purple sofa,
cruising around the room
on the rest of the furniture,
letting go for a second or two
to retrieve her board book.
And I can't shake the feeling
that as I sit here watching Daisy
I am watching the recapitulation
of the creation of the world
and every human life

And what is it in my *Baybuhgirl*,
in any child,
that makes her want to,
need to,
stand straight up,
let go for a second,

and one day stagger off
across the toy-littered floor
looking so mightily
pleased with herself?

What is it that leads any one of us
to dare what we have never done,
embark with unsteady legs
and tentative steps
on the pathway of
our own unknown?
What is it that drives us,
motivates us
--such mortal creatures—
to risk our limbs, our backsides,
our heads, and our hearts
makes us stretch out,
leading us forward to become?

I'm still watching Daisy.
She keeps standing there alone,
her knees wobbling
turning over in her hands
that board book
she just dared all to retrieve ....
when suddenly
with a look of gleeful fulfillment
she sinks her two little teeth
deep into the delicious book's spine.
And boy, does Grammy laugh!

Perhaps the great human motivator
for all things,
whether worthy or unworthy,
can be summed up that simply:
We risk all
because
we WANT.
Or at least we want a taste.

Daisy's Big, Wide World

To give her stay-at-home Daddy
a sanity break
to go mountain-biking,
and to take an active part
in my only grandbaby's life,
I have been babysitting
Daisy one day a week
for all of the eleven months
since she was born.

At first I was all too aware
how long it had been since
I was a new mother
taking care of Daisy's Daddy.

So you say you burp them now
by sitting them up on your thigh,
with one hand supporting
under the chin and
across the front of the chest
while you pat the baby's back?

And show me again how to
snug up these diapers
on this long-tall-Sally
of a girl and fasten these things
that don't have any pins?
And does the picture
on the diaper--Winnie-the-Pooh,
has anyone considered the irony
of this character's name?--
go in the front or the back?

It took me months just to learn
to strap on the snap-this–into-that,
blue-slide-here-red-slide-there,
button-clicking, buckle-tightening,
crossover-the-shoulder-and-back

baby-carrier without help from my son
before he would leave the house.
It's a wonder Daisy's parents
left her alone with her Grammy
for even a minute, let alone a day.

But Daisy has survived me
and proven herself to be just
a bit of a *wild* flower,
crawling early, a climber,
going up the stairs
by herself at six months,
shoving her high chair
and two stainless-steel,
step-on recycling cans
around the kitchen
before she could walk,
walking at 10 months,
causing gates to spring up
in front of the TV and stereo,
at the foot of the stairs,
at the entry to the kitchen,
with Daisy even now
seeking out toeholds in the gates,
figuring out how to scale them.

I have loved all my days with Daisy,
but yesterday was the most wonderful yet.
After lunch I grabbed Daisy's
pink tennis shoes with
white-organdy-ribbon bows
and put them on her feet.
I slathered her with sunscreen
and plopped her pink hat on her head.
I've carried Daisy around the block,
toted her in the ding-blasted baby-carrier,
pushed her in the stroller
and in the chariot that hitches
to the back of her Daddy's bike.
But this time I carried Daisy out the door

and set her down on the sidewalk
on her own two feet.

And Daisy took off at a stagger-toddle-run.
No holding Grammy's hand.
No looking back, just running pell-mell,
oops, down, then up and running again,
bruisingly fondling flowers,
pointing up at the tops
of the breeze-blown birch trees,
squatting down to crunch
crispy leaves in curious fingers,
lying down on a gravel path,
making a dusty "snow-baby"
as she scuffled her feet and legs
and arms and hands
back and forth in the stones,
deliriously absorbed
in pure experience.

The whole, wide world is Daisy's now.
I am so happy,
feel so lucky,
I was there one day
when Daisy ran out to meet it.

My Inheritance I Give You

Sometimes I take it out of memory
like a family heirloom, velvet-wrapped,
turning back the corners
of midnight-blue cloth
to reveal, say, a silver spoon,
a topaz brooch,
a string of pearls,
or pewter candlestick,
my inheritance
from my Great-Grandmother,
Mama Brown.

But my inheritance is neither spoon,
nor brooch, nor pearls, nor candlestick.
It is a name.
My Mama Brown called me
Dear-To-Love.
First grandchild,
first great-grandchild,
little girl with wispy hair,
the apple-pear-and-peach
of everyone's eye.
A three-word name:
such a treasured gift
given to me by my Mama Brown
when she called me Dear-To-Love.

I have my own first grandchild now,
and her own sweet name is Daisy,
but I call her by other names, too.
Sometimes she's Nay-Nay,
because those were her first
wailing words as a newborn.
Other times I call her Baybuhgirl,
or Sweetie-Girl, or Biddy-Bump
just because I'm crazy about her
and showing her with crazy names.

But here before me sits my inheritance,
so recently taken from memory again,
and I realize I want to hand down
this family treasure to my grandchild.

So Daisy, I'm writing this poem
to say *all* the names I give you
say how much I adore you.
But I especially want to bequeath
to you my own blessed name,
Dear-To-Love.
Every time you hear this name
or any of the many others
by which I've called you,
may each name remind you
how very much your
Grammy loves you,
and how loveable you are.

Daisy in the Garden

The reunion photos
tell the story of our
grand-daughter Daisy,
not yet two, on her first visit
to the family farm in Ohio.
Here's one of Daisy, barefoot,
in blue shorts and top
in Aunt Molly's garden,
hunkered down
behind magenta zinnias,
having just plucked
a small green tomato
from the vine,
biting into it
as if it were an apple.
So this is how small green
not-appley things taste!

Here's another:
Daisy, barefoot again,
is lying on her tummy
on the damp earth
between the garden rows,
her legs kicked up,
her little feet and toes
wonderfully grimy
and poised in the air,
her hands burrowing down
a hole in the garden soil
as she turns toward the camera,
grinning her pearly-teeth grin.
…then one second later,
wriggling her body
and pressing belly and cheek
delightedly down on the dirt
as if snuggling against the earth.
So this is how the body of the world feels!

In yet another photo
in Aunt Molly's sun-soaked garden
Daisy is picking up a baby pumpkin
still attached to its vine,
finding its underside
mud-caked,
studying this
and the dirt
now on her hands.
So this is a wondrous warm orange thing
with dirt on it and a long green string!

And just one more snapshot
for good measure:
Daisy with her blonde curls,
wearing blue bib-overalls
and a white shirt, standing
in front of a white picket fence,
rubbing noses with Sadie,
Aunt Molly's ever-so-tolerant,
ever ecstatic and loving white lab.
So this is how this doggy
and a wet nose
and a summer day
and joy
and safety
and freedom feel
when you're a Daisy in the garden.

Grace

My husband and I arrive
to spend the day with our
two-year-old grand-daughter.
Daisy, full of delight, crows,
"Papa! Drammy! You're home!"
At lunchtime we all head out
to the Mexican restaurant
where Daisy and I have partaken
of beans, rice, corn and cheese
since her age was calculated
in double-digit months, not years.
Daisy tucks in,
skimming off cheese to eat first,
picking up slippery kernels of corn
with her fingers and placing them
daintily on her spoon for transport.
Mid-meal, she unexpectedly stops and
reaches out to take her grandfather's
index finger in her left hand,
then to me, to take my index finger
in her right, nothing more, just that.
Everything and everyone else disappears
as we watch and wonder
at this little girl,
just quietly sitting,
not saying,
claiming us
with her sticky-fingered love.

Daisy, Not Napping

At almost three, Daisy has started
pre-school three mornings a week.
I'm so interested in her new little life
outside our seeing and hearing
that I ask her questions she
doesn't know how to answer yet...
"Tell me about your school," I say.

But this is not a school day,
and Daisy's Daddy has left saying,
"Daisy has to take a nap—no excuses.
If she doesn't lie down and close her eyes,
leave the room until she complies."
For Daisy, sleeping alone is bizarre,
cruel, inhumane. She has always had—
and thinks she must have—a warm,
cuddly, loving someone sleeping
next to her right in the same bed.

We try to nap. Grammy is very tired.
But Daisy somersaults and tumbles,
turning over and around and back
more times than a dog trying
to make a bed in a thicket of briars.
I remind Daisy of what Daddy said
about napping...
And trying to live up
to the boundaries set,
I leave the room
when Daisy hasn't rested
or even come to rest
in the first half hour.

Three times I get up to go,
and each time Daisy gets frantic.
"Don't go, don't go. I'll sleep," she says.
But when I come back to bed--
Grammy *really* needs a nap now—

Daisy lies still for about 15 ½ seconds
then resumes her tumbling and turning,
flinging out a silky scarf,
trying to lie down fast enough
that the silky scarf will cover
her before it hits the bed.

After a very long time of this
non-stop, rigorous not-napping,
I sigh and roll on my side
to look at Daisy, thinking,
What are we going to do with you?
She rolls on her side, too,
to look at me,
beaming blinding rays
of cuteness
and how-can-you-resist-me?
"Hi, Grammy," Daisy says.
"I love you…
Tell me about your school."

The Lion-Shaman

I am sitting up in my hospital bed,
the world no longer spinning
at quite the same rate it was
when I came in here through
the ER two days ago.

I hear my grand-daughter Daisy,
almost three now, in the hall
and wonder as I hear her voice
if she will be afraid of this place,
afraid of or maybe afraid for me.

Daisy hasn't seen me since
my son, her Daddy, drove me
through rush-hour traffic
to the emergency room
with Daisy asking
in a worried little voice,
"Grammy, what's wrong?"
while I'm retching
into a purple puke bucket,
unable to open my eyes
lest I see landscape and cars
traveling faster than I was,
spinning off to my right
to my right, to my right
a carnival ride gone very bad.

I experience a little bubble
of joy knowing Daisy is here
and am glad she'll have
the chance to see that
though people get sick,
they also get better.
And now here Daisy is
in a summery cotton dress,
her hair pulled up
in two little ponytails that

look like blond question marks
on either side of her head.

Daisy comes to the foot of my bed,
assessing, giving me one of her
I'm-looking-into-your-soul-now stares.
Then she hikes herself up on the end
of my bed and on hands and knees
starts to crawl up the length of my body
like a lion cub practicing stalking prey,
one hand-knee-paw down
and then, cautiously, another,
not speaking at all, her eyes on mine,
her eyes doing all the talking.
"Is this okay?" they say, "Are you okay?"

Daisy makes her way from my toes,
to my shins, my knees, my thighs,
my hips, my belly,
all the way to my chest,
where she stretches out
her lion-cub neck,
kisses me on the lips,
then snuggles her head
in the hollow of my neck.

If only the pharmacy
could bottle this.

Mammories

I'm crossing the parking lot
to our favorite Mexican restaurant,
carrying my little grand-daughter
on my left hip. Her right arm
is resting on my shoulder,
her fingers just inside the
neckline of my sweater,
skin-to-skin.

Suddenly she breathes out
a rapturous sigh
and exclaims with wonder,
"I just *love* my mama's boobies!"
I laugh out loud and say,
"Yes, you really do!"

This little girl may be weaned
but she is harboring mammories…
of the silkiness, the warmth,
the cuddly bliss of sinking
into pure sweet momminess….
into what her mommy once
christened the "squirty pillows."

Daily Lessons

*For Shulamit Hoffman
and Viva la Musica!*

Singing Christmas

We have been singing Christmas.

A chorus of various and sundry angels,
we began appearing unto one other
every Monday night
not quite four months ago.
Our labor has been long
and sometimes painful
as we have struggled
with foreign tongues
and rhythms
to bring to birth again
the story
of this dear child,
this Great Love,
as it is told
around the world.

In these four months,
we have learned to lean
into one another for comfort
during twinges of dissonant harmonies.
We have counted and timed together
the tempo of our musical labor and rests.
We have swaddled each other
with words of encouragement,
shared laughter and the mutuality
of the sometimes excruciating reality
of the task we had taken up.

And at last the day did come
when we sang Christmas.
It was in the very sacristy that
we fixed each other's hair,
pinned on sashes and boutonnières,

whispered our anxieties,
checked our music,
smothered our laughter,
shooshed each other's talking,
and gave praise for the small miracle
of one unlocked bathroom.

Then into the hush of all those gathered,
we came forth to give all we had to bring.
With guitar, piano, harp, and bass,
with drum, marimba, and flute,
we sang of olives, of raisins and honey,
of the Holy Child and the Holy Mother,
of holy light, and a holy dance.
We sang our glorias, our alleluias,
our doo-bahs, and our la-la's.
We even shook our ya-yas!

And when we were done,
in the midst of the bows,
ecstasy, happiness,
peace wrapped me 'round
like a heavenly balm.
My heart was enormous with joy,
wanting to embrace every angel
around, about me…
wanting to kiss our Archangel Shu
right on her smoochy lips…
wanting to dance for joy
with each person in the audience,
because the Lord of the Dance
still goes on…dancing in us.

There is no wanting in me this season
no longing, nothing left out,
no other gift needed.
I am filled up with love.

…For we did well and truly
sing Christmas to birth again.

Bill Gates Doesn't Love Words

Dear Bill,

I heard a report that you are once again
and still the wealthiest man in the world
with an unbustable titanium lock on the
computer market. While I'm sure that's all
very nice, I feel I must tell you, you are flat
broke and chintzy when it comes to words.
In fact, I believe you may not even like them.

First of all, there's the problem with the name,
Microsoft <u>Word</u>, just one <u>word</u>.

Right away that doesn't bode well for writers.
When we writers are looking for just the right
word to express exactly the nuance we want,
Microsoft's bundled thesaurus is lifeless,
impoverished, a mobius strip of suggestions
all turning back on themselves, everything
self-referencing. No vistas opened, no bells
of recognition rung. No inspired leaps of
connections that lead to witty word-play.

Bill, Bill, for word-people that just isn't good
enough. Writers want to poke about in gaudy
flower markets of words with blooms in so
many varieties we go giddy with the choices.

We want to rummage in hodge-podgey antique
stores and flea markets of words where we may
chance upon a find: quirky words, dusty words,
small gems for which we may find new uses.

We want to wander about exotic word bazaars
looking for treasures hidden inside little fringed
tents and under canopies held up by sticks.

We want to dive deep into rough-walled blue grottos where strange, phosphorescent words live.

We want to make the trek to the word mountain top to see all the way from here to where our words might take us next.

I could download someone else's thesaurus from a website or purchase separate thesaurus software at my local techie store. I could even access some big, clumsy thesaurus-rex on the internet. But I don't want to have to reach so far when I'm in the middle of a thought. I prefer a more intimate and immediate meeting with my words. When Microsoft Word disappoints me, I find myself taking down from the shelf my trusty old Webster's New World Thesaurus, its cover half-ripped off, its pages yellowing, its copyright date 1971. A ratty old book that still gives me more than your Word.

Bill, Bill, you can do better than this. Throw some money at the problem, this dearth of kindling-wood words that spark ideas. Put some programmers on the project who love language. Refashion your thesaurus with creativity, imagination, and some mind-stretch. We don't care how much money you make; all we writers want from you is word riches.

Word-hungry,
Ann

Impersonating Elvis

I saw him on the sidewalk
outside the theater
and knew he must be the actor playing Elvis,
hair dyed an uncharted shade
something darker than black,
cupie-doll hair curling down just-so
upon his forehead,
collar flipped up, shirt open down to there
and no chest hair,
rub-on body-bronze (or freakish tan)
bordering on orange,
boots with heels, jeans breaking over
turned-up toes.
And he wasn't in costume.
These were his street clothes.

We went in when the theater opened,
for the Sunday matinee and took our seats
for the only musical of the season.
When the house lights went down,
Elvis made his entrance, and sure enough,
our man-on-the-street Elvis was also
the Elvis on-stage.
Such a line-up of Elvis hits
to knock out he had,
and he knocked them out one by one
being very Elvis,
smacking his guitar, swiveling his hips,
striking Elvis-like poses,
his back-up band rocking
while my eyes were rolling
as I got ever more squirmy, creeped out,
and wiggy in my chair.

I love theater…
and Elvis was one of the home-boy,
sex-toy, heartthrob icons early in my era.
I was *watching* the Ed Sullivan show

the night they blacked out
the lower half of TV screens
across America to keep Elvis-the-Pelvis
from corrupting the nation's youth,
for doing what came naturally
to a black-and-blues beat:
pelvic thrusts, thigh shimmies,
undulations, and gyrations.
Yeah, I saw it all. So what was it about
this Sunday-matinee idol Elvis
that was freaking me out that day?

At intermission I hung out
with what was bugging me
instead of the crowd in the lobby.
What must that be like…
walking around every day of your life
inhabiting some other person's persona,
wearing Elvis hair, Elvis skin bronzer,
Elvis attitude,
practicing in front of the mirror
so you could stand on stage
hitting each memorized,
studied and rehearsed
Elvis-move just right?
Now I slap the strings,
now I dip my guitar,
now I shake my pelvis,
now I twist on one foot,
now I thrust my hips
just like this…1, 2, 3 stop.

In the second half of the show
I looked around the room
and realized
no one
was being transported
to rock-and-roll heaven ,
or moved to dance
in their seats

or the aisles.
No one was rocking out...
except the back-up band
and secondarily the guy
who was impersonating
Elvis rocking out on stage.

The thing is I just wasn't
getting anything very Elvis.
It's not that the guy was
a bad Elvis impersonator;
he had it all down.
It's just that there was
nobody home in *his* body,
none of *his* life energy
exploded on the stage
or grabbed us with
something now
or new or real.
Who would this guy
be if he weren't
every live-long day
impersonating Elvis?
What would *he* wear?
What about *his* hair?
How would *he* sing?
How would *he* move his hips?
How would *he* live
if he were himself
not a copy of somebody else
who was but isn't...
and certainly never will be
this Elvis-come-lately other guy?

After the mandatory Elvis-big-finish,
all the obligatory bows and clapping,
followed by—what else?—an Elvis encore,
I walked out of the theater musing:
Why had I choked and gagged
on this performance

like it was a fish bone?
Anything that caught me
with this much barb
must be lurking somewhere
in my own nature, too.
Don't we all need to do
impersonations sometimes,
putting on what we know
will be the best face for
the Highway Patrol cop
walking over to the car…
the doctor who's going
to perform our surgery…
the loan officer who's
holding our application…
the manager we hope
will hire us…
the boss whose neck
we'd like to wring…
or *name your own*
 impersonation
situation here?

I thought: The only thing that
saves us is remembering
we're *not* the person
we're pretending.
Because if we pretend
anybody long enough,
we forget who we are,
the true Self dies
and we go on
pathetically
impersonating Elvis.

Too Much in the World

When it has been weeks,
or even months,
without a poem,
I am too much
in the world.

When my eyes are
blurring, strained
from looking outward,
I am too much
in the world.

When my body hungers
in such a frantic way,
when my limbs are limbs,
indeed,
when exhaustion
hangs on me like
a cloak of wet sod,
when tears hover
and the glimpse of
copper-colored cows
on green hillsides
until now unknown to me
bring down those tears,
I am too much
in the world.

Shall I then kill myself
a little more today
with tasks and errands,
spending, wasting, running?
Body, my spiritual practice,
Body, my spiritual teacher,
you let me down, again,
making me let go, again,
so I fall out of the world, again,
and into the arms of Creation.

Bad Week

They find dry-rot in the pergola,
then in the support beams,
then in the siding of the house.
Then the shower door shatters
into a trillion tiny, shiny pieces
and I'm standing naked,
ankle-deep in broken glass.
Then the washing machine
breaks down mid-cycle,
leaving a load of clothes
to steep like teabags
in the tepid tub.

Just in case I hadn't noticed,
a few cosmic hey-you's…

It's not just the pergola;
my spirit is dry, without substance,
riddled with fibrous, crumbly holes.

It's not just the shower door;
I shattered a relationship with
ill-timed and reckless words.

It's not just the washing machine;
I can't seem to rinse or drain,
can't let go of what is no use.

What was it the angel-messenger
with his name stitched on his shirt said
when he'd fixed the washing machine?

"These things are vulnerable like that.
Don't let the lid slam down fast and hard.
Take time to close it slow and easy."

Hey, you. I get it.
Hey, me.

Ugly Dog

Oh, you are an *ugly* dog,
body and head jammed together
so you look like a bullet with legs,
fur so dull, dark, mottled and mangy,
you look like you need some Rogaine.
You skulk—a creepy word,
because you *are* creepy--
along the edge of the ravine that runs,
scrubby and undomesticated,
just north of our rows of townhomes.

It's early morning,
and I've been out walking
while you've been out skulking.
Now we are passing each other
in opposite directions
on opposite sides of the street.
You hug the edge
of the underbrush
and give me the evil eye
across the narrow divide.

Oh, you are an *ugly* dog.

And as you pass me
in sinister silence,
not a bark on your breath,
but tailing me with your eyes,
I realize you actually are not
an ugly dog out skulking…

you are a coyote
being your perfect coyote self.

What If…?

I've always been a reluctant flyer,
the kind who's suddenly seized by
a compulsion to update her last will
and testament at the boarding gate,
the kind who walks
the jet way to the plane
like a plank off a pirate ship.

Don't try to confuse me with
logic or rationality or any
unbelievable statistics about
auto-accidents vs. plane-crashes.
My vacation inspirations *always*
turn to nervous perspiration.
We're going to France!
Maybe we shouldn't go to France.
I don't want to go to France.
Let's stay at home, on solid ground.

So my husband now has reservations
about making any reservations,
concerned that one day I will brace
myself in the jet-way door
and just say no,
causing us to lose out
not only on the wonders of the trip,
but also all the money
or frequent-flyer miles
we've squandered on those
damnable, non-refundable tickets.

I hadn't planned to change,
didn't know I could.
But then, just before leaving
on a flight to go see my family in Ohio,
a Trickster-thought rapped
a tickling tattoo on the inside of my head:
What would it be like to be someone

who isn't afraid of flying?
What if I were to pretend I am
someone who isn't afraid to fly?
I laughed as Trickster/Shape-Shifter
stuck out his tongue at my fears and
waggled his fingers up-side his ears.
And then…pretending is just what I did.

I pretended myself to the airport,
through check-in,
through *three* security checks--
I suspected they suspected
I was actually someone
who is afraid to fly--
then pretended myself onto the plane,
pretended myself into my seat,
pretended to be unaffected by turbulence
or any strange grinding,
thumping, or screeching noises.
Instead, I read and ate and slept
and watched the lovely ant-world,
its snaking mountain ridges,
its dollhouse towns,
its geometry of fields,
the silver threads of its rivers far below.

It was sighingly lovely. I really loved
being someone who isn't afraid to fly.
And why was just pretending enough?
Maybe because I have been consciously
making peace with my death,
trying to come to terms
with the fact I actually *will* die
either now…or in the future,
either in the air…or on the ground.

If I can pretend I am not afraid to fly,
what else could I begin to pretend
that might become the truth?

Perhaps, if we let it, the rigidity of the
ego-self will begin to wrinkle, soften,
and melt like our flesh and our skin,
as we age, a kind of reconstitution
of the malleability of our clay,
allowing the Creator to continue
working in the studio of creation,
making us realize who we thought
we were is not necessarily
all we can be.

Fetch Me a Lick of Sense

It is late afternoon,
and my friend, Catherine,
and I are walking
in the scrubby flats
just inland from the ocean
with her brown Labrador, Lela.

Lela tears out in front of us,
racing away, racing back,
bounding around us in circles,
her entire body wiggling,
wagging, zigging, zagging,
begging Catherine to throw the ball,
throw the ball, throw the ball, please!

Just a few feet down the dusty trail,
Catherine drops Lela's
green tennis ball on the ground,
claps over it the cupped end of this
long, green plastic ball-launcher thing
called a Chuck-It,
picks up the ball with the cup,
and with a practiced throw,
swings both ball and launcher
back over her shoulder like a tennis pro,
flicking her wrist at just the right moment
in the down-swing
so Lela's tennis ball sails
        up and out and away and away.

Lela, nearly wild with joy,
her paws scrambling in the loose,
dusty sand at first, like some cartoon dog
trying to get traction,
goes streaking after the ball,
across the sandy moonscape,
traveling so fast
she catches the long ball

on the first bounce.

Over and over, non-stop—
her body hugging the ground
and curves like a sports car--
Lela races after the ball, grabs it,
and races to drop the ball
at Catherine's feet,
which I gather in Doglish means:
Throw it again! Throw it again!
Out-and-back, over and over,
until, just when I think
Lela will play this game forever,
she brings the ball back at a slow trot
and stands at Catherine's feet, waiting,
but also refusing to give up the ball.

I haven't played fetch with a dog
in a long time, and I have to ask
Catherine what Lela is doing.
Catherine says this is what Lela does
when she's tired; she keeps the ball,
won't give it back until she's had a chance
to rest and catch her breath. I laugh!
Because it doesn't look easy to pant
and let your tongue hang out like that
when you've got a grubby green
tennis ball locked between your teeth.

Catherine and I stroll on along the trail,
content in our walking and talking
with Lela trotting quietly behind us.
Suddenly, Lela appears in front of us,
and, splot, the ball hits the sand,
which in Doglish clearly means,
"Here, person; here, person,
heave the ball out there again."
Catherine sticks the cup on the ball,
hoists the ball on the Chuck-It,
and flings the ball out to never-never

where Lela races away to hunt-it-up.

And all I can think is,
Oh, Lela, I want to be like you!
I want to inhabit my animal-body
so entirely that I know when I'm tired--
without guilt or resentment or judgment--
possessed, instead, by an animal-wisdom,
that stays me, makes me wait and rest,
holding and holding and holding that ball—
the one that always feels
like it's in *my* court—
firmly in the grip
of my own sharp teeth.

Crash Course

I signed up for a crash course
on being a mystic...
and crashed, of course.

It started this November,
after a lifetime of hints and innuendos
and the occasional bolt of lightning
or 2 x 4 whacked upside my head.
I was out walking after a rainstorm,
spinning in an inner whirlwind of desire,
so passionately yearning to learn
to practice the presence of God
in all the moments of my life
and not sure how it needed to be done,
when, but for the blink of an instant,
my *I* evaporated and God looked out
at the damp and dappled world
through my eyes.

Oh, Holy One! Oh, My Beloved!
We humans are Godholders!
And I went home and gave to God
myself so God could write a poem
about the ecstasy of intimacy.

Seven days later I was driving by a
bus stop and caught a blinking glimpse
of a teenage boy in over-sized clothes,
a knit cap pulled low over his eyes
and was pierced by his loneliness
and his despair
in a way that was a prayer.

Oh, Magnificently Creative Life Force!
Oh, Compassionate Presence,
you are here with me in every now.
And I went home and gave myself
to God to write a poem-prayer

on behalf of that young man.

I was destined to be a mystic.
I was God's own,
and I would never forget.
Look at me, look at me!
I'm learning to practice
the presence of God.
Three days later I crashed,
clearly practicing the presence of Ann.

It was in Macy's Men's Department
where I had gone to return a shirt.
The shirt was new; washed once
before I noticed a slub in the fabric,
a discolored knot of thread
smack, dab and obvious
right in the front on the pocket.

I held out to the Macy's sales clerk
the receipt and this freshly laundered,
freshly dried, never-worn shirt.
The sales clerk looked at the receipt
and her cash register read-out and said,
"You've already returned this."

What? "No," I said,
showing her the shirt again,
"I'm holding the shirt
right here in my hands."

She examined the receipt
and the register once more,
"No, you've already returned this."

Had logic left on Thanksgiving vacation?
"No," I said again, "See."
I brandished the evidence in my possession,
gave her a forced, gargoylish
Miss-Congeniality smile,

indicating I was trying to patient
though she was very clearly WRONG.

But again she looked at the receipt
and reiterated for the 93rd time
the impossible, illogical,
jackass-ian pronouncement,
"You've already returned this shirt,"
this shirt I was holding in my hand.
And I detonated.
Almost before I knew I was going to do it,
I slammed my fist down on the counter,
and shouted, "Goddamnit.
Don't say that one more time.
I'm holding the damn shirt
right here in my hands;
how could I possibly have returned it?"

Nearby shoppers stopped where they stood,
like somebody had hit
"pause" on reality TV's VCR.
A great hush fell upon Macy's.
After several awkward-as-storks-on-stilts
moments of silence, the clerk said,
"But you see, you've already re...
um...well, the best I can do is
credit your card for...uh, $31."
The shirt in my hand,
the one that matched the
SKU number on the receipt,
the one exactly like piles of others
marked $49.50 on a nearby table,
had cost $49.50.
But that, of course, was the shirt
she was sure I had already returned.
$31 was the cost of one other
shirt listed on the receipt.

My eyes flashing like chili-pepper
Christmas tree lights,

I bit off the word, "Fine,"
and spit it out in a tone
that clearly meant not-fine.
"I guess I'm going to
have to settle for that."

By the time I walked out to my car
I was an embarrassment to myself
and worse than that,
I was an embarrassment to God.
I didn't deserve to be a Godholder.
Today, instead of evaporating,
my *I* had inflated to fill
Macy's Men's Department,
all three floors of the store,
and the Sunglass Hut next door.

I drove home, picked up the phone,
tracked down the clerk in the
Men's Department, asking for the one
who had just had an encounter
with an irate customer
in a bright red sweater,
and I apologized,
saying I was an
embarrassment to myself,
that we were talking
just one human to another,
and she hadn't deserve
the behavior I'd exhibited,
that I hoped the rest of her
holiday would be better,
with no more ill-tempered customers
like the one in a bright red sweater.
Thank God she didn't say even once
that I'd already returned the shirt.

In seminars thirty years ago,
we were continually reminded that
just about the time you're starting

to feel beatifically spiritual
and full of only righteous goodwill,
...just about the time you feel you're
reaching some new pinnacle
of enlightenment,
some direct line
to God on High,
you step in dog crap.

That's just to remind you you're human.
That's just to remind you to be here now
and pay attention to what you're doing.
That's just to remind you
that every sales clerk,
every phone call, every stabbing pain,
every sadness, every joy, every relationship,
every place, every moment of every day
is an opportunity
to practice the presence of God.

And now, dear friends,
if you'll excuse me,
I must bid you adieu
and go to practice
the presence of God
while cleaning dog crap
off my soul and my shoe.

She'd Rather I Were Lying

In my imagination she sits
in a chair beside me,
her arms folded across her chest,
burning me with a high-voltage glare.
She is the "other" part of myself,
the one who has been of late
so regularly short of patience,
tart of tongue, judgmental,
provoked without provocation,
poised to go mental at every moment.

"What is *wrong* with you?"
I ask this nasty part of myself
that embarrasses me, makes me sad,
the one who acts like I don't want to act,
the part I would gladly cut from the cast
of my inner characters if I could.

Her eyes say if she were a cobra
she would rise on her tail now to
spit venom in my blue-green eyes.
 "I am the price you pay for being tired,
for running yourself into the ground
every day of your bleeping life."

I baulk and go hard, glaring back.
"I don't want to hear that again!
I'm sick of living with my body's
ridiculously limited boundaries,
sick of being constrained in what I can do,
tired of having to measure out my life
by the thimbleful and ¼ teaspoons."

"Fine," my nemesis says,
"Then I'm what you get.
Run your life any way you please.
But if you're tired,
I will be speaking for you

and acting for you,
and smashing and thrashing
about in the world around me
with a studded cudgel."

There's no way to fake her out.
or shake her, or disregard her.
When it comes to my body,
this part of myself
won't let me
lie
to myself
when she knows
what I really need
is just to lie-down.

The State of Things

**War Poem for a Little Girl
in a White Dress**

As I came downstairs this morning
I could see the Special 8-Page,
All-WAR section of the
San Francisco Chronicle
lying on the breakfast table.
Even before my foot
touched down on the last step,
your image burned my retinas.
From clear across the room
your face was screaming in terror,
fire and black smoke billowing up
to singe the sky behind you,
shock-and-awe bombs
chasing you from your home,
rattling your teeth,
hammering you like a fist,
giving you night terrors
for how many years to come?
If you live.
And I can't stop crying.

You are only—what?—
three or four years old.
I am thousands of miles away,
but I can feel your heart pounding,
I hear you crying out,
your mama, mama, mama words
on your tongue,
crying out for her,
your grandmother,
your father or brother,
for your anyone,
for me,
crying out as your people flee
the fire, the bullets, the bombs
with no other destination than "away."

Who dares call you by the name
"regrettable collateral damage?"
You are a little girl
in a white dress
so incongruously
and innocently ruffled,
your dark eyes terrified,
your black hair flying away,
your face contorted
with what anyone can see
is not shock and awe,
but a little child's pure,
bone-liquefying terror.
I see you and feel
so angry, so powerless
in the face of the whole world's
governmental, political madness.
And I can't stop crying.

You are someone to me.
I feel your soft skin,
feel you bouncing on my hip as we run,
feel your fingers clutching my clothes,
hear your terrified cries.
You are someone's child,
God's child,
my child,
my grandchild about to be born
in another time and place.
And I can't stop crying.

Darling Girl, oh Darling Girl,
where can you run to?
Run to my arms.
Run to my heart.
Run to my tears.
Run to my prayers.
Run to my poem.
It is all I have to give you.

Heads-of-State Grudge-Match

Surely war comes out of some
dinosaur part of the human brain,
a Paleolithic, Neanderthal
approach to problem-solving
we haven't quite given up or
found a workable substitute for yet.

But it has suddenly occurred to me
that the Comedy channel on cable
just might have a solution for us.
From their bizarre, irreverent brains
has come "Celebrity Death-Match,"
a weird cartoon in which ugly little,
claymation models of celebrities
get into the ring and fight
to the comic death.
Sound funny? Surely not.
But in some outrageous,
absurdist way it is.

So I'm thinking, why not world leaders?
Let's keep the soldiers alive and well at home,
let civilians stay in their unbombed houses,
save the holy places, the antiquities,
the infrastructure and the architecture,
and keep our nuclear weapons holstered.

Instead, we give the heads-of-state a time-out,
lock them in a room together
and refuse to let them leave the place
until they reach a creative solution.
Let them go ahead and act-out all they please…
Refuse to speak or negotiate,
Call each other nasty names,
Bore each other to death with speech-ifying,
Take up arms--and hands--against each other,
Re-draw maps,
Sleep it off,

Kick each other's butts.
Days, weeks, months, years?
It doesn't matter.
They don't get out until
they've figured it out.
Nobody gets hurt.
And all it costs is
delivered pizza.

Being Seen

We park on the street
in a seedy, commercial/industrial
area of San Francisco on our way
to an evening of small-stage,
even-smaller-crowd theater.
I step out of the car and onto the curb
in my long, iridescent raincoat
and high-heeled boots,
with my short, blonde hair
and my French perfume.
Immediately a black woman
of indeterminate age is at my shoulder--
a street person, I can tell, by the
stiff, cardboard-colored blanket
she's clutching around her.
She's literally in my face;
her eyes, their whites so white,
searching my face as if mine
holds all the answers
and all the available light.
And for some reason,
I am not afraid of her.

She asks, as if it might be so,
"Are you the mayor?"
I grin at the thought and tell her no.
She's walking sideways beside me now,
her body turned toward me
staying as nearly shoulder
to shoulder as she can get.
"I need to git me a hotel room.
Can you gimme some
money for a room?"
I know there is a lie in this,
but it is so cold on the street...

Our eyes are on each other,
hers and mine,

our vision locked-on
like laser-guided missiles,
like we've fallen into
some kind of eyeball spell.

I say, no, I'm sorry, I won't
give her money for a room.
I don't say it automatically,
like I might,
but as if she and I are actually
having a conversation as I keep
walking toward the theater,
as she keeps walking sideways
right beside me.
I don't mind her presence,
but her eyes are disconcerting,
they are so…on me.

"You don't really have to gimme
no money for a hotel room," she says.
"Jus gimme money for a drink…
I'll pass out anywhere."
I look at her and say,
"Boy, you're really telling
the truth tonight, aren't you!"

Just then a voice behind us scolds,
"Tha's rude!
She shouldn' be doin' like she is.
Tell her to go on
to the women's shelter;
…it's up there jus round the corner.
She got no call to be doin' like that."
I turn to see who's speaking
and find behind us
another woman who looks
to have been walloped
to within an inch of her life
by fate and her choices…
teeth missing, skinny, stringy hair,

clothes that tell stories of hard nights.
One street person chastising another?
For the sake of protecting me?

My blanket-wrapped companion heeds,
stops where she stands, shuts her mouth.
My husband and I cross the street,
leaving her on the corner.
I look back at her.
She keeps following me with her eyes,
no malevolence, just locked on,
wanting something.
Wanting something more,
I am sure,
than just a room or a drink.

Of Hawks and Doves

In the first week of January, 2003
…as hawks and drones,
spy planes and war planes
zero in ever tighter on
intended targets in the Middle East
…as our newspapers, airwaves, and
brainwaves boil over with the scalding
rant of war and holy-terrorist scenarios
of madmen armed with chemicals, gases,
poxes, plagues, and nuclear missiles
…as we lean less toward de-fusion and
diplomacy and more toward baiting
lethally-armed, delusional leaders
with our talk of pre-emptive strikes
…I am doing nothing more significant
or useful in this mad-mad world than
undecorating the Christmas mantelpiece
in my home in safe and sunny California.

For several days I've had
this picture in my head,
this urge to sweep away the cranberries
and branches of cotoneaster,
now wizening and drooping
with post-Christmas exhaustion,
to put in their places a rustic birdcage.
A bird cage? Yes, something in me insists.
A bird cage I bought on an impulse
months ago, not a bird to my name.

I clear the mantle of berries and branches,
leaving two small candles
with electric flames.
I wipe the marble mantle top clean,
set the wood-and-wire birdcage
on the far right,
stand back and look,
taking in the cage,

the opulent briar wreath,
the mirrored wall above the mantelpiece
…and realize immediately that
something more is needed.

From the top of the armoire nearby
I take down two fat, white, wooden doves,
a long-ago gift from my mother.
I put the doves in the cage
and fasten the doors closed again.
I stand back and look once more.
But still, something more is needed.

On the left, I add a tall, green metal urn
and fill it with a spiky, exuberant fan
of dried leaves and flowers,
then a shorter green-glass vase
holding a bouquet of dried hydrangea.
I stand back and look once more.
But still, something more is needed.

Ah, here's an idea then! What about this?
I walk over, unlock and then throw open
the doors of the birdcage,
as if to free the doves to take flight.
It is then the symbolism hits me,
and I am blind-sided by grace:
The doves of my mind's eye
and my insistent imagination,
these mythic, winged messengers of Spirit,
need to be freed
to flee the cage, fly out,
and come back to us with olive branches.

Standing in my home, before the fireplace,
arranging flowers, vases, and a birdcage,
I now realize I'm making prayers,
a holy place in the soul of my home,
a ritual of lovely, newly-consecrated things.
And surrendering to this tug of inspiration,

my heart has suddenly burst open,
letting white-winged hope and faith
fly forth into the wearied, worried world,
freeing and letting loose in me the certainty
that an olive branch will come back to us,
a green sprig of promise, assuring us
if we free the caged doves within ourselves,
cataclysm and destruction need not be
our destiny or the destiny of our planet.

This, then, is what I can do, all we can do:
follow the tug of inspiration,
fall on our knees,
write the poem, walk the dog,
light a candle, take out the garbage,
sing canticles of longing,
write letters to our leaders,
splash exultations of color on fresh canvas,
create altars in our kitchens,
bring forth a new rhythm on the drum,
reconcile where we're called to,
march in the streets,
dance in our living rooms,
be present in our work, kiss our beloveds,
bear witness to the beauty and fragility
of our wondrous world,
every person,
every creature in it…
do everything we do
as if all our living were a prayer,
because all our living is.
Free the doves.
We must free the doves within ourselves.
For on our own internal vision
rests the future.

Driving by a Bus Stop

I'm driving on El Camino Real,
that blaring, bustling, busily
anonymous urban street.
I am passing by a bus stop
and catch a glimpse of a young man
of middle school or high school age,
wearing big, baggy jeans,
a big, baggy coat,
and a knit cap pulled
down low on his head.
He's sitting on the bus stop bench.
I see him only for an instant,
in my peripheral vision…
but my breath catches in my throat;
tears well up in my eyes.

Something about the angle at which
this young man was holding his head,
something about the weary, weighted
slump of his body,
telegraphs his despair,
his hopelessness,
his loneliness,
his emptiness,
a reflection in the dark
looking-glass of my own
long-ago depression.

Is this what it is
to fall in love with God?
When I begin to step out of
the center of the universe
and do whatever is asked,
when I try to give myself up
for God's self-expression
in the world,
is this what I get?
These tears in my eyes

for a young man I don't even know?
Evidently so.
But the question that skewers me is:
How can God possibly use me?
What can God create or express
through me
on behalf of this
lone, lost manchild
at the bus stop,
when all I have to give God
are my lifetime of experience,
my limited stamina,
and my poems?

And God takes my experience
and my limited stamina,
and writes you this poem
about hearts laid bare
everywhere,
so your noticing
becomes a prayer,
even at bus stops
when you're driving by.

For Amanda

The Devil Takes All

Was that the Devil
sitting just inside your door?
Was that the Devil
who reached over and
swung the scabby door open
because I was knocking,
tilting his head back and
leering at me upside down
with his meticulous black beard
and smiling/frowning lips
on the top of his head?
Was that the Devil who
in that same instant exposed
       you
on the couch in a dingy slip
or maybe a nightgown,
worn under a new black T-shirt
that in Goth/ic type said "Sex"
on the sleeve and something
I can't quite remember on the front.
Was it "emancipated,"
which you clearly are not?

You jump to your feet
when you see me
standing in the doorway
of this apartment where
you're currently crashing.
You jump up so fast,
you knock over a beer
which runs away from you
to puddle under the couch,
and you almost yell at the maybe-Devil,
"I told you not to open that door,
no matter what."
Even though you knew,

probably because you knew,
I was coming.
Don't you remember...
You told me you'd be here?

I quickly step back out of the doorway
onto the gritty walkway of the building,
still holding my grocery bag of
co-dependent food, wondering
what should happen next..
And something about the maybe-Devil;
that dark, cramped room; the way you look;
the way you won't look at me
tells me you recognize
the place you're in
as a bus-station on the dark side of hell,
makes me think I may know now
how you're getting your drugs
when you are so totally broke,
when you are so totally broken you'll
trade the Devil his crank for your sex.

Your voice is dead, weighted with hopelessness,
as you say from inside the apartment,
"You might as well come in now.
The damage is already done."
Not knowing what else to do,
I step back through the doorway.
You're sopping up
the beer with a bath towel.
But we both know
that's not the damage you mean.
The real damage in your mind is that
I've seen you in this circumstance at all,
that I've seen the black-haired Devil-man,
walked in on your physical extremity,
witnessed your vulnerability,
grasped the fullness of your
twisted gift for self-destruction.
The thing is, you think

I didn't already know.

I see now that you can make the Devil
disappear for at least a little while.
And I wonder where he is now.
Slouching against the wall
behind the bathroom door?
Flopping back on an unmade bed?
Peeing in some dark corner
to mark his druggy territory?

You stand in front of me,
and for once in your life,
have nothing to say,
you of the dazzling mind,
the cunning charm,
the words, words, words,
and the multitudinous excuses.

I know you're coming down
from four days of "tweaking"--
as you tell me tweakers call it--
four straight days of crystal meth,
four straight days and nights
without sleep or food.
You told me this on the phone
when you called again,
crying again.

You look like hell,
your eyes utterly exhausted,
because drugs are a trick
the mind plays on the body,
making you think you are in ecstasy
while you're committing suicide
by needles, pipes, or lines.
And though the ravages of all that crank
are in your face, I'm shocked to see
that without your Goth-girl makeup
and dyed-black, black, black hair,

you look young, so innocent,
even with all your face jewelry
still sticking out and through.

I hand you the bag of groceries.
And I hug you.
You are not able to look at me,
but I feel you falling into my embrace
with your whole suffering self.
And now I ask the wrong questions,
Do you want to give me the pipe?
Can you give your body
even just one day off,
so you can make it to your interview
for that rehab program?

You look at the floor for a long time
and then whimper, "…I can't."

And I get it.
And that's when I first begin to know
I won't be coming to you like this again.
And I hear a certain dancing wise-woman
whispering in my consciousness that
we must all back off twelve steps now,
because the good we're trying to do for you
isn't doing you any good.
You don't need rescue-rations,
unending understanding,
more praise for your intellect and creativity,
or somebody to cry on when your uppers have
brought you crashing down.
These things don't help, let's face it,
because all you really want is
another piece of the Devil's candy.

But you don't really know this yet…
or that if you don't die to this life soon,
you will surely die from it.

Brilliant, desperate, despairing, slashed, burned,
crystal meth and pot-smoking woman/girl,
the problem is not your terrible childhood,
though it was terrible.
It's not your psychiatric diagnoses,
though your diagnoses are complex.
It's not that you are so special and unique,
though you are.
The biggest problem is you are an addict,
lying-in-the-gutter average,
a street junkie like any other.

All the wisdom of the age says the best
we can do for you now is let you go,
giving up our rescuers' need
to save you,
allowing you, finally, to free-fall.
Because unless you are allowed to
fall
all the way
into of the ruins of your one and only life,
into the full terror of the Devil's quicksand,
you probably haven't got a prayer.
Not any prayer but ours.
But we will pray it without ceasing.

Suicide Bombers

They blow themselves up.
They're blowing themselves up.
They're exploding, immolating,
fragmenting, splattering
t h e m s e l v e s
and their   ha p pe nst a nce
victims
across the wide landscape of hatred.

What brings a young man
to kill himself like this,
so brutally?
What causes him
to scorn
the pleasures of
all his tomorrows:

all the unsavored meals,
all the unlaughed joys,
all the uncheered soccer goals,
all the undanced music,
all the unseen nights full of stars,
all the unprayed prayers,
all the unbuilt businesses,

and the unkissed woman
who might have been his wife,
the unembraced souls
who might have been his children?

What brings a young man to choose, instead,
to take a ritual bath,
to shave his body,
to anoint himself with scented oils,
to chant prayers as his teeth chatter,

then fly a planeload of grandmas,
sales reps, CEOs, teenagers, dads,

infants, moms, tourists, spouses,
people,
just people,
any people
into a building,
exploding their humanity
in a ball of fire…

or to board a bus and blast
every just-someone on board
to kingdom-come…

or to walk into a café,
a market square,
a Passover Seder,
any public place
and detonate the shell that is himself,
dying savagely…
to make what point?

And does he reach paradise then?
And does he find 28 virgins waiting?
And does he see God?
And what does Allah say?

What internal forces work
in the minds and hearts
of young men,
that they are able to
gird and arm themselves
generation after generation,
that they can run each other
through with swords,
lead a charge on hell's own hill,
storm a machine-gun bunker,
fight hand-to-hand with knuckles,
knives and bayonets,
assassinate the assassins,
crush buildings, homes and people
under the tracks of tanks?

What in their genes, in their genders,
in their hormones
gives them the stomach
or the guts
to risk their lives,
to lay down their lives like this?
Does their DNA spiral like a
barber pole around the terrible
stake of "noble causes"?
Is the fight for survival of their own kind inborn,
demanding the role of
valiant knights and savior-warriors?

But they're blowing themselves up.
These young guys are
blowing themselves up.
Blowing themselves up.

And one hideous day
the carnage crosses the gender lines
in one future-cidal leap.

And suddenly young women
are strapping on ordnance,
blowing away their hearts,
their breasts,
their wombs,
their brains,
their consecration of life,
humankind's entire roadmap
to the future.

What has happened that
young women
are blowing themselves up?
Once we were the mothers crying
No! as our sons went off to war.
Once we were the ones left
to wail over the senseless
loss of our children and

the men we loved.
Once we were the ones
keeping track of the disappeared.
Once we were the ones pleading
for sanity in insane times.
Once we were the
keepers of the future.
Now these girls are
blowing
themselves
up.

And does an eighteen-year-old girl
ritually bathe and ritually shave...
does she ritually anoint herself with the scented
oils of eternity...
before she walks
to the grocery store
and blows herself up,

taking anyone—
even just one other
anonymous teenage girl—
with her
when she shatters her flesh?
An eye for an eye,
a tooth for a tooth,
a pound of flesh...
if there's that much left.

They're blowing themselves up.
Actually blowing themselves up.
And what do these
young women expect?
Do they think they
will be transfigured
into paradise?
And what good will
28 virgins do them?
And will they see Allah?

And what will Allah say?

They're blowing themselves up.
These young men and women
are blowing themselves up,
as an act of hopelessness,
as an act of desperation,
as an act of martyrdom,
as a sacrifice for their people,
as an act of war.
Their actions mean they see no way
to a better life
than death
by dynamite,
by plastic explosives,
by crude fertilizer bombs,
and taking with them
as many of those who are
not-them
as they can.

And when those who are not-them
are a people nearly annihilated
by mass murder once before,
now being wounded and killed
at   random
in their own homes, streets, and stores,
is it any wonder their tanks thunder out
to strike back?

And I don't want these kids
to know it works,
it's true,
I notice the war, the mayhem more
when it comes into my living room,
lands on my breakfast table,
one exploded young man,
one splattered young woman,
one blown-away market square,
one demolished café,

one-two fireball skyscrapers
at a time.

They wanted to make a difference.
They wanted to make meaning.
They wanted to force a change.
They wanted to be valiant and noble.
But now any chance they had
is over...

Unless those of us who are left
allow their shattered, splattered bodies
to shock us into truth.
Bring it home.
Smear it in red on our mirrors.

Where in my hidden self
do I hold the grudge
I will not let die?
Where do you?
Where am I
keeping score about
who did what to whom first?
Where are you?
Where have we deafened ourselves
to the others' cries,
blinded ourselves
so we don't see
their suffering?

Wipe the mirror clean.
There's nobody out there
but us.

For our children,
for all our children,
let us bear witness
to the explosive reason
these kids are dying
and make haste...

Let us rush into the crowd.
Let us gather Hope in our arms,
Let us lay Hope down in the
middle of the war-wracked street,
tip back Hope's head,
and resuscitate Hope,
breathe life into Hope
and breathe Hope back
into the future.

These kids
are blowing
themselves up.

The Zen of Ants

Sometimes ants bug me.

They come traipsing in my kitchen,
somehow taking it over completely
with their little tiny selves,
not even seeming to have a good idea
exactly what it is they want.
This time they're in the sugar bowl,
next time in the butter.
Now they're ganging up
on a dried-up brownie crumb,
swarming an innocent sponge,
or dumpster-diving in the waste basket
for no apparent reason.

When I was younger,
in my twenties or thirties,
just one single-file column of ants
was enough to send me to the phone
to call the exterminator
and get him here right now,
or even sooner,
to spray with ant-icidal poisons
so all those ants would die, die, die.

But as I grew older, perhaps wiser,
and more measured in my responses,
when I found armies of ants
marching on my kitchen,
I just set out discreet, little ant traps,
or made concoctions of boric acid,
or zapped them with Windex,
or Hoovered them with a Hoover.
I didn't call the exterminator.
But make no mistake,
I still wanted those ants to die, die, die.

It's winter again in California now,

and armies of ants have broken
and entered my domain once again.
But I have grown yet older,
perhaps yet a little wiser…
And I find I look at the ants a bit more
benignly now, saying to myself,
They'll go away when the weather changes,
you know…in whatever way ants
need the weather to change.

So I practice sharing my kitchen.
Ants in my wastebasket?
It's all right; I was done with that stuff..

Ants in the sugar bowl?
Dump the sugar in the wastebasket
and be done with that, too.

Ants in the upstairs bathroom?
How *did* they climb all those stairs!

I practice sharing my house now,
surrendering to what is
right in front of me,
co-existing more peacefully
with reality,
seeking enlightenment
by practicing
the Zen of ants.

For my Wise-Woman

What To Do After You've Seen the Wizard

In the Land of Oz, Dorothy had her Wizard.
But in the Land of Soul, I have
a Wise-Woman,
a most creative and blessed companion
who has been sitting across from me,
our knees nearly touching,
at least twice a month
for more than ten years.

In all that time my Wise-Woman
has been wise, indeed,
comprehending my words,
both spoken and unspoken…
walking with me through times of
physical, emotional or spiritual distress…
abiding with me in the garden
of my soulwork…
inviting me to open ever wider the door
to my inner life and my dreams,
to dive ever deeper into sacred depths…
encouraging my poems, my art,
every kind of creative expression…
sustaining me on the manna of ideas,
books, quotes, stories, scriptures, poems,
images, symbols, laughter, and dance.

But recently, War was preparing
to break its flimsy chains of dreads
and threads and spider webs and escape
to slash and burn and bomb the world.
And when I went to see my Wise-Woman
I was dragging in with me a body bag
of human outrage, heartsickness, jelly-legged
helplessness, and raw, nail-bitten despair.

But War was in the room with/in both of us.
This time, these times, when I went to see
my Wise-Woman, I could not find
useful direction in our connection,
for she, too, was carrying
the same sorrowing in her soul.
Sometimes she couldn't seem to help
but say that she ached for the human family,
brothers and sisters all, yet ready
to bomb, burn, and batter one another.
She couldn't seem to help but mention
a peace march she'd been part of,
a kneel-in where the names of the dead were
read over rows of small caskets painted white.
She couldn't seem to help but express
her concern over the calamities we as a country
might be calling down upon ourselves.
She couldn't help but shake her head
over the impaired vision of our leaders
who seemed blind to any course but War.
The smooth white moon of her face
began to gray beneath a cloud-cover of fatigue.

At home, I found I took to watching religiously,
and I mean that word exactly,
a news-show parody
that used humor like a sharp stick to poke holes
in policies, egos, and hysteria alike, making me
laugh 'til I was nearly sick.
With relief.

And one day, as I was getting ready to leave,
I found myself quietly saying
 to my Wise-Woman:
"You need to laugh."
"Yes, we need to laugh," she replied solemnly.
Ah…but "you" and "we" and "I"
were not the same.
And suddenly it happened:
I saw the Wizard.

A light bulb snapped on backstage,
backlighting reality's fragile scrim,
revealing not the Wise-Woman
I had always seen before,
but a beloved and very human companion,
someone who looked and talked and felt,
in fact, a lot like me.

So what do we do when we've seen the Wizard,
when the pedestal we've hand-carved crumbles,
when the star we've hung falls from the sky,
when the valentine arrives postage-due,
when the prophet profits but does not save?

This is what happened when *I* saw the light:
I felt calm, grounded as granite…and wise.
Knowing I would talk with my Wise-Woman
about "you," and "I" and "we" another day,
I gathered up my purse,
the wisdom I'd come in with,
and ten years' worth of powerful projections.
My Wise-Woman didn't need to carry
my projections or my wisdom anymore;
I was strong enough to carry them myself.

For Amanda

Broken Things

Sometimes when I see a broken thing—
a shattered water glass,
a splintered mirror—
I know it is not salvageable,
can never be repaired,
restored to wholeness again.

Yet when I look on other broken things—
a snapped twig,
a cracked tibia
a fractured relationship—
I know it may take time,
but the wound or injury can be healed.

From the day I met you, your chaotic energy
has caught me up, spun me, exhausted me.
And looking at you I could never be certain
exactly which kind of broken you were,
smashed by life, to be sure,
but irreparably so? I could not say.

Tonight is Maundy Thursday.
You rush up before the church service,
wanting to share your latest poem.
I read the poem aloud to you
as you ask me to
and find it—and you—
more lucid,
not so purposely or unwittingly obtuse,
totally entangled in your own brilliance.
The poem is about the miracle
of seeing a new therapist,
one who isn't from the often
oxymoronical governmental
mental health system,
one who is wise in transpersonal soulwork.

I know this new therapist.
I know she won't simply pathologize you,
despite your wretched, wrecking past.
I know she will see you
as a beautiful being,
in some ways broken,
but one whose pieces all remain,
one for whom the daunting task of
integrating all those pieces
is not an impossibility,
but a spiritual quest,
a life's task of the highest worth,
to help you seek and reconstruct or find
the Priceless Perfect Jewel
at the center of your Self.

You want to sit beside me in the service,
so we take the second pew together.
I go to the pulpit to read a scripture early.
You go forward to read the very last.
I look at you reading with such feeling.
You are dressed in a long black skirt
and a long black top,
with a scarf around your neck,
your hair black and vivid purple,
the studs and rings in your lips and tongue,
and your eye makeup glittering,
your eyebrows shaved…
but you are beginning
to look like an adult to me.

At the end of the service,
all light extinguished,
Jesus' death on the cross is marked
by the tolling of a doleful chime,
one stroke for each of his 33 years.
You reach out to clutch my hand.
I feel your tension the entire length
of your body as you sit
beside me in the pew.

Our pastor has asked the congregation
to leave the service in silence,
so as we exit I wordlessly motion you
outside to the veranda
to stand with me in the falling dusk.
I put my forefinger to my lips
and whisper, "Don't say anything."
Without planning to,
I find myself taking into my hand
the ankh —
that ancient Egyptian symbol of life —
you're wearing.
I hold onto it as I whisper to you,
"I want you to know I see
you are serious about your healing.
You are healing.
And you will be healed."

We embrace.
There are tears in your eyes.
I think I know what kind of broken you are:
The Easter kind.
The kind that can be resurrected.

I Want To Turn Away

There they are marching
in single file down the hall
or displayed on the living room wall,
or hung like a gallery in the bedroom.
Does anyone in the house
really notice them anymore,
these faded photographs
of babies and children,
new high school grads,
grooms and brides?
I may never have met
the people in these pictures,
and yet I feel so uneasy
when I come upon them
that I want to turn away.

It has happened so many times,
I've come to recognize the
nature of my dis-ease
...I don't like to notice how the
browning photo paper divulges
how many years have passed.
...I don't like to see how the
long-gone-to-Goodwill clothes
tell, in their fashion, poignant tales
of once upon a style ago.
...I don't like to let in the way the
hairstyles in their tortured oddness
record how even *now* will one day
be yesteryear, out of step and quaint.
I am still *now*, I tell myself.
Then I think, honestly, not quite.

This week after long hesitation
I am hanging on our bedroom wall
two framed photos of our
two-year-old grand-daughter
whom we so dearly love.

I wonder how I will see these images
in a year or two or ten or more?
Will I see only the fading,
how time has flown
or limped away?
Or will they simply recall that lovely
summer reunion on the family farm
when she was not yet 2 and I was 60?

I have decided to hang
these sweet photos in our bedroom
as they do prayer flags in Tibet,
prayers printed on flags of paper
hung out in the elements,
meant to be ravaged by time
and sun and wind
until they fade, fall to tatters,
and disappear,
their prayers and goodwill
having been blown on the wind
by then and spread to all the world.

So there you are
on photo-paper prayer flags
which time will no doubt dim,
my darling Daisy.
But whenever I look at you there,
in whatever years have passed,
may I experience the rain of blessings
of having had you in our lives
for whatever years have passed.

Consumed by Consumption

Spiritually, I'm stranded
in the Valley of Dry Bones,
arid
parched,
isolated,
desiccated,
nothing left of me but dust.
But our cupboards are bare.
We need, at the very least,
the stuff of stone soup.
I drag myself to the super market,
prop my carcass on a cart.
I go shopping.

My ship of purpose has gone down.
I cling to a twig,
treading water, and treading,
and treading, and treading,
exhausted from all this
staying in one place.
But it's Christmas.
There must be presents for all.
I crawl to the mall,
avoiding any Blessed Undertow.
I go shopping.

Inert, uninspired, dim-witted,
dull, I languish inside
my cobwebbed, rusty armor,
my brain a dried pea
rolling around in my skull.
I'm either waiting to die.
...or perhaps already dead.
But we need new
lamps for the bedroom.
So I shuffle and creak
to Lamp-R-Us.
I go shopping.

Life whispers to me:
What you need is: color, beauty,
refreshment, creativity, all manner
of ravishment for your senses.
So why is it the acquisition of
faux-suede purple pillows,
lamps that glow from within,
a strand of glittering beads,
a bag of fresh oranges,
a bunch of star-gazer lilies,
a tin of 70%-pure-chocolate candies
has such a short shelf-life,
soon leaving me in need again?

Look inward, shopper…
A poem knocks faintly at my door,
but I'm not there to hear it.
A little creative make-thing
peeks in my window
looking for me,
but I'm too tired,
too busy, to see it.
A continual parade of
one-time-only possibilities
arrive on my doorstep.
all dolled up just for me in
get-ups of diamonds, chicken wire,
broken mirrors, flannel, jelly beans,
sack cloth, Silly Putty, lace,
bunting or alligator shoes
with live alligators.
Such a rich inner world of
beauty and creativity
is mine to mine.
But I'll never find
what I truly need
if I'm not even home
when it tries to find me.

For mother Amanda, baby Antonio, father Jesse

Little Redeemer Child

Savior,
Redeemer…
Such weighty words
to lay upon a babe so small.
But not for you, little one,
the saving of all souls,
just this one:
your mother's…
who for you finally cracked her addictions,
who for you finally fled homelessness
and made a home to lay your head,
who for you finally took care of herself
so the authorities would have no reason
to take you away when you came.
In saving you, this sweet new life
she made with your father,
your mother is saving herself.
In your coming,
little black-haired redeemer child,
you are saving her

Beloveds

Retiring Early

So many nights now
you go to bed before I do.
Of an age to retire,
but not yet retired,
you have to compensate
by retiring early each night.
I come to bed a little later.

On this night, too tired to read,
I turn off the light,
slide down
into the cozy envelope
of flannel sheets and soft blankets.
You are breathing rhythmically, slowly,
having already tumbled down
into the eiderdown of sleep,
I turn toward you in the dark,
find your face with my hands
and kiss you lightly on the lips.

Your hand,
I cannot see,
but in the next moment
I feel it,
skin-to-soul,
warm upon my cheek
…feel your knuckles
trace my jaw line softly,
…feel the pad of your thumb
come to rest,
gently pressed
against my lips
like a seal.

I am suspended in one of those
I-could-die-now moments,
die young, retire early from my life,
without regret.

To be touched so,
to be loved so,
without a word
is, for me, the Holy Grail,
all I could need
or ask for
in this life.

For my amazing daughter-in-law Darcy

**Hard-Hatted Woman
with Band-Aids**

Our daughter by marriage is
a woman with more resources
than the seven continents combined,
mines and mountain tops, rivers and
underground pools, fields and forests
of resources within her she's had
to draw on to face more than her
share of bruising hard times in her life.
What she's got to do, she does.
What she seeks, she finds.
What she suffers, she heals.
What she desires, she acquires.
Given a spark of hope and enough time.

What other woman do you know
arrives at her big interview for the
Information Technology Manager
post at a mega-construction company
carrying a field-engineer's clipboard?
Wearing a regulation hard hat?
With her name printed on it?
And puts that hard-hat smack
on the interviewer's desk so her name
is staring him straight in the eye?
She got the job. We're not surprised.

But our daughter-in-law's resourcefulness
extends far beyond her gutsy-ness
to matters of the soul and the heart...
When she decided the time had
come when she must wean her
toddler daughter from the breast,
she knew she couldn't face the task
unless she could somehow turn off
the mother's-milk tap without

leaving her daughter in distress.
Her resourcefulness kicked in and
soon had her in the bathroom taping
Band-Aid X's across each breast..

That night when her daughter
came calling, ready to crawl
inside her mother's shirt,
mommy pointed out the Band-Aids
and said what she knew
her daughter would understand,
"Mommy has owies. Broken."
Her empathetic toddler drew back
with concern…but accepted that
the squirty-pillows she loved so much
were off-limits, that they didn't work,
were, sadly, broken.
In the night, when her daughter
nuzzled for a drowsy sip, our
daughter-in-law whispered,
"Remember? Owies…broken."
Her baby girl gave a disappointed little
whimper but then went back to sleep.

But it was after this when this resourceful
woman's resourcefulness was truly taxed,
when she had to go inward and dig deep…
the day she took the Band-Aids off
and her daughter asked hopefully, "I eat?"
What a treasure of diamonds, coal, oil,
gold, timber, and rain forest secrets our
resourceful woman had to lay down then
…when she had to make herself say,
"No, that's just for tiny babies.
And you're my big girl now."
…when she had to let her baby go
so the rest of their life together
could begin.

The Five-Minute Kiss

I say to my husband
as we stand hugging
in the kitchen
so I can keep an eye
on bubbling pots
and melting butter,
"I told the acupuncturist today
that my energy seems better,
but my libido is still
pretty much the same.
Dr. Wong said changes
in libido take a long time."

"That's the problem!"
I say to Larry.
"I take a long time!
I want-to,
and I want to want-to,
but my body somehow
keeps forgetting how."

Larry smiles his
wiser-than-a-monk smile
and backs me up
against the nearest wall,
pressing his body into mine
in the way he knows I love.
He doesn't try to fix
what he knows he can't fix;
he just "gets" what I'm saying,
just-getting being something
he's gotten remarkably good at
after all these years.

That night, after dinner,
after some snuggled-up time
watching a funny video,
Larry shuts off the TV,

takes off his watch,
pushes some buttons,
and lays it on the coffee table.
 "Okay," he says, "I just set
my alarm for five minutes.
We're going to kiss
for five minutes
without stopping.

Go!"

And he pounces on me
and presses his mouth to mine.
And I start laughing;
my lips are laughing,
and he is kissing my teeth.
And I laugh even more
as I'm trying to say
through smooshed lips,
"Oh, how dear...how sweet!"
And I'm laughing
in my belly
in my throat
in my chest,
love bursting in me
like toy balloons
full of diamond glitter,
I'm hugging him and laughing,
still failing at a proper pucker,
when, with his lips still pressed
against my mouth, Larry says,
"There seem to be a lot
of teeth in this kiss."
And I laugh so hard my teeth part,
and he kisses me with his tongue,
and I answer him with mine.
And the alarm goes off.

Seems I have time-release libido.
I go off two nights later.

Crying Over Enchiladas

We sit across from each other
in a favorite Mexican restaurant,
having established beforehand
that it's not the night for mariachis,
so we can talk.
She is tall, beautiful, and casually
elegant, the kind of woman who
can wear white canvas Keds
and make them look nonchalant chic,
the perfect accessory to go with pearls.

We order, hand over our menus,
and launch into our life stories,
connecting deeply and immediately
as women so gloriously, naturally do.
And we start the process laughing…
because when I say
I wanted to get to know her
from the first time I saw her in church,
she says she thought the same of me.
And we each admit we had
admired the other's hair,
surely the basis for a long
and meaningful relationship
if ever there was one.

She's eating her enchiladas,
and I, my fajitas,
when she comes to the part of her story
that encompasses now…
the breakup of her marriage of 12 years,
the distress of her young children,
the years her now-almost-ex became
ever more irrational and threatening,
as she closed herself in,
closed herself down…
until it became almost normal
to feel nothing at all…

until the verbal and emotional abuse
threatened to become physical,
making her numbness more dangerous
and her brother, to shake her awake,
said, "He's a big man. What are you going
to do when he really comes at you?"

It shocked her. In a detached way. Intellectually.
Like in a movie she was watching
about someone else.
But enough that she registered
the very real possibility of danger
and began to take steps
to move out of his life
and into her own…
the hardest part being sharing
the children and the piercing
realization of how shell-shocked
her children already were.

Throughout this gritty
domestic horror story
of diminishing self-esteem,
spikes of stress and fury in the house,
the fabric of life woven with meanness,
her dulled senses and emotional deadness,
her fear for the children and then herself,
she has remained dry-eyed.
I imagine myself into her life,
and I say, "I bow before your courage."
And now her first tears fall.

"I don't know why I'm crying,"
she says, wiping her eyes
with her napkin, embarrassed.
"These days I start crying
for no apparent reason.
I don't know how I could
get through all those years
and then start crying now--

when it's nearly over.
Sometimes all someone has to do
is say something kind."

She doesn't know why she cries yet,
but she will.
She inspires herself.
Right now the woman
who is making these daring changes
seems like someone
she used to know,
a friend of long ago
she'd nearly forgotten.
She cries because she's
moved by her own courage,
moved to claim herself as worthy,
moved by giving birth again
to her own high-spirited Self.
For years,
the whole enchilada (of her Life)
has been crying out for salt.
So...

May she let all her tears fall,
fall as they will now,
for they will restore to her
her Life with all its intended,
deserved, delicious spiciness,
its full saltiness and savor.

My Racy Corvette

When we were young,
our passion ran fast and hot,
our engines revving so quickly
we could go from 0 to 60,
-- well, fast, really fast! —
and peel out (or off) together
like a couple racy Corvettes
...if you know what I mean.

In middle-age maybe the
0-60 times we clocked
weren't quite so fast,
but our engines still raced,
and our timing was great.
We just had to warm up
my classic Corvette a bit
and travel in the
not-so-fast lane...
where we found
it was now possible
to enjoy the scenery
as we drove
unswervingly
to our destination
with our top
(and bottom) down
...if you know what I mean.

But now we're past 60...
60 years, not miles per hour.
And while we still take
pleasure in going
out driving together...
it's not like it used to be!
What I'm driving now
is a *vintage* Corvette
that sometimes
has trouble getting

its engine started.
My aging auto is still
something of a beauty
in a heavy fins-and-chrome,
well-used sort of way.
But if you want to get
the best out of the old girl
now you've got to give her
kidskin-driving-glove
treatment.

You have to sweet-talk her,
pat the curve of her fender,
tell her she's looking
mighty sexy for such
a well-traveled car,
let her know ahead of time
you're thinking about
taking her out for a spin
so she has time to remember
she's not up on blocks
in the garage
for the rest of her life.

Going out driving in
a vintage Corvette
can be fun…
sweet and quiet
and intimately lovely.
Mostly she'll get you
where you want to go,
not fast but slow…
except on the
occasional night
when *nothing* is working
and all I am thinking is,
Who installed this
damn Denver Boot!

For my mother, Louise Beattie

Spicy Mama

When we were kids,
we had a spicy mama.
She'd eaten at Johnny Marzetti's
restaurant and learned
her garlic lessons,
at least one bulb
in papery white skin
always waiting in the cupboard,
ready to be peeled and crushed
for soups and stews
or rubbed on the rare—
I mean, occasional—steak.
Our mama's pasta sauce
was garlicky, too and
thick enough to grab hold of
even the most slippery noodle.
Her chili was con carne,
also con onions, garlic,
and lots of chili pepper powder.

Our spicy mama's life was spicy, too,
always up to her elbows in soapsuds,
pots and pans, dirty clothes, or little kids.
Taking care of a houseful of seven,
she was a one-woman shuttle service
to and from cheerleading practice,
basketball practice and football practice,
attending our sports and music events,
managing the Boosters Club banquets,
single-handedly putting on
big parties in our small home
for my father's colleagues
and his football players
from the college,
everything done up down-home style:
with homemade buns and pecan tarts,

ears of sweet corn by the platterful.
Our mama may have been exhausted,
but her life was so spicy
and she was never bored.

Now our mama has turned eighty.
X-rays of her spinal column
show something that looks
like crumbling Greek ruins.
Her hip gives her pain when she walks.
She's takes good care of herself;
and she has to…she's diabetic
and needs medication for
several other diagnoses
so many of us face as we age.

Sometimes when I'm back in Ohio,
visiting, my mother and I sit on stools
at her kitchen counter and delve deeply
into the subject of aging,
how she's dealing with it,
things that make her happy,
like having kids or grandkids drop in,
things that are hard,
like not being able to do all she once did,
things that make her sad,
like feeling isolated and out of the swim,
about what's missing from her life,
and that always adds up to one thing: *spice*.

Sitting at the counter with our cups of tea,
my mother laments how little she can do…
…then tells me about a local ministry,
pre-supposing they wouldn't be
interested in someone who is eighty
who would like to volunteer as a
receptionist for a few hours a week.
…discusses the welcome baskets
she makes for visitors at her church.
…numbers over 2000 the greeting cards

she has created on her computer,
the same computer on which
she writes the minutes and official
letters for her condo association.
…and nods when I mention
the water colors she paints
and that she practically
reads the library dry of fresh ink.
Still, too often, to her, her days taste flat.

There in the kitchen as I am talking
with my mother, I know
I am also talking
with my future self.
In my own way
I've been a spicy mama, too,
even a red-hot mama at times,
if I remember right.
I adore the pungent spiciness
I've found in abundance
in writing, singing, dancing,
in good books, good food, a good man,
and the blessing of so many rich
and well-seasoned relationships.

But being 70 or 80 or 90 changes things.
Will I find a way to exercise a little,
even dance, when I walk with a cane?
Will I find I can still write with passion
when my world shrinks
and all I have to write about
is my ever more inward life?
Will I be able to call my life good
if my good man dies first?
Will I feel it is enough when what
I can do best for those I love is listen?
Will I feel cherished and worthy
when someone else cooks my meals,
helps me change out of the blouse
dotted with the bits of breakfast

my eyes can't see?
Will music bring me to an
ecstatic state when it's
something I listen to more
than something I can make?
In my age, will I hunger for spice?

At lunchtime, my mother and I go
to her favorite restaurant, Chipotle.
She orders a Mexican Burrito in a Bowl
and splashes her spicy food all over
with green Tabasco sauce.

Don't Take This Away from Me

"Don't take this away from me,"
the former-jock says to his parents
with quiet fierceness
from his now-permanent seat
in a wheelchair.
His parents only meant
to shield him from
further pain and suffering,
but it is of his pain and suffering,
he says so heatedly:
"Don't take this away from me."

It's just a TV show,
but the young man's words
stick in my mind
like Crazy Glue.
The words will not let go of me,
stay with me all night
until I hit upon a memory:
My mother so lovingly asking me
if I wanted to come home to Ohio
"to rest and look up at the big trees"
all those years ago
when I was lost
in the dark wood of depression.

As lost as I was, as tangled and dark
as those woods were,
I knew I could not go home.
Though I couldn't have said why, then,
now I think I know…
In some deep and secret part of me,
I think I was trying to claim my life
as my own, saying even
of my despised depression,
"Don't take this away from me."
In the months that followed,
it was my depression that changed me,

saved me,
revealed to me
the fullness of both Who Am I?
and the great I AM.

"Don't take this away from me,"
the young actor said on TV,
and days afterward,
his six scripted words
still stick in my brain.
There is something more
calling to me in these words,
wanting to come into life.
And I keep connecting
the dots of intuition
until I come upon
a more raw, unformed,
and troubling link:

Outside the TV in my own life,
I am the one who wants to
shield my loved ones from difficulty,
help them solve their problems,
take away their pain and suffering.
I know I can't, but even if I could,
I have a most disturbing sense now
what a disaster that would be.
Don't take this away from them…
Only walk with them,
remembering
it is in the very struggle
with what Life brings us
that we may be blessed,
delivered from flimflam falseness,
healed into wholeness.
Don't take this away from them.
But it is so hard, so very hard
just to stand with them, loving them,
watching them as they struggle…
Maybe this is how God feels, too.

For all the many—too many— wounded women

Bird with a Broken Wing

They reach out for each other
in the darkness,
feeling for each other
--are you there?
For months she has been
lost to him
in the downward-dragging
quicksand of her past,
he, in the wilderness of losing her.
Tap, tap—are you there?
Do you know who I am?
Do you remember someone else
you thought was me?
Will you love me if I tell you
how I feel about myself,
that I am ruined?
Tap, tap--
Hand meets hand,
but no light breaks.
Fingers entwine.
"I miss you," he whispers.
"Is it okay?" he asks after a time.
"No," she says, "I'm scared."
Scared, she means, of allowing
now
what she didn't get to say
she didn't want
and couldn't claw and fight off
then.
In the darkness his fingers
softly touch her face, her hair.
He is gentle, without demand.
She reels herself out to him
timidly,
slowly,
inch by vulnerable inch.

Perhaps she can begin
to allow this now,
knowing his touch
may be healing
because he knows now
just whom he is loving,
the true All of who she is.
Perhaps she can dare
to begin allowing,
knowing her allowing
may be healing,
proving to herself
her body is her own
and in giving her
in-all-ways-naked self
to this man
what has held her
prisoner for so long
will begin
to lose its power.
They tremble within and without
at the enormity of the moment
before them.
"There is no hurry," he says,
knowing as he never has before,
the privilege that is her body,
when it can be freely given.
Her eyes fill with tears
deciding whether she can
yet offer him herself.
His eyes fill with tears
knowing now the strength
it must take to take back the past,
what trust it must take
to rest in his arms--
a small bird
with one broken wing
and the survival instinct
of twelve hundred tigers.

For my valentine, Larry

Warms His Hands, Too

It's an evening ritual,
sometimes an afternoon
and a morning ritual, too.
Something tells me it's
time to set the water to
heat in the electric kettle.
I warm a pottery mug,
swirling hot water in it
as the kettle bubbles
and burbles,
then clicks off
with a final ta-da!
I pour boiling water
over the teabag I have
waiting in the mug,
Twinings Earl Grey—
Oh, it *must* be Twinings,
and it *must* be Earl Grey,
and it *must* deliver *caffeine*--
so I let the tea steep for
a good long time,
until the tea is
coffee black.
Finally, I toss the tea bag
in the trash and carry
the steaming mug
to my husband
wherever I may find him--
at the table reading the paper,
in the office on the computer,
in the TV room watching the game,
in the garage cursing Styrofoam.
We gingerly transport
the red-hot mug
from my hands to his.

He always thanks me.
He always looks both
surprised and pleased
to receive the tea,
though I've made this
same delivery hundreds
of times through the years.
A small, domestic,
servant-like act?
I think not.
Last week,
on February 14th,
my husband came up
behind me as I stood
washing a few dishes
at the kitchen sink.
He put his arms around me,
and whispered in my ear,
"Every time you bring me
a cup of hot tea,
it feels like a valentine."

*For the cherished, truly loving person
who forgave me this grave transgression*

On Not Saying

In the middle of the night,
I sometimes say things that
would not get passed my lips
or fingertips
in the middle of the day.
After-words, I wish there
were a "Take Back" button,
or that e-mail would
precipitously devolve,
get un-invented,
so henceforth I would have
to toil with pen in hand
for long, unwieldy hours,
address the envelope,
affix the stamp,
and walk my message
to the mailbox
the morning of the next day…
every step along the way
a chance to regret my words,
to stop,
take it all back
--home--
and sit on it
until I'm sure
this is what I want to say
and how I want to say it
or if I should say it at all.

E-mail makes it too E-asy
to empty tear-ducts and
spleen at the keyboard,
and with one click "send"
my troubled, too-tired,
raw or red-hot words out

into the unsuspecting night.

When I am sleep-starved
in the middle of the night,
I'm a crazy lady, unbalanced--
chemically and every otherwise.
I am a sixty-year-old two-year-old,
too tired to sleep,
fried, frazzled, tortured, tearful.
Little dragonflies of distress
turning into reckless dragons
spewing slime and fireballs
out my mouth and hands.
Secrets and ugly things I
usually keep locked up seem
to have no night-shift jailers.
They break out, get loose
to trample people and landscapes
in their big black, chain-gang boots.

Awake in the middle of the night,
I am jangled, unhinged, deranged,
on the edge…
not the clean, bright,
discerning
edge of a scalpel,
but the jagged, rusty
edge of an old tin can lid,
one capable of inflicting
nasty wounds that pain and fester
with even one quick unintended nick.

"Don't send any e-mail in
the middle of the night,"
my husband counsels.
"Revisit it in the morning…wait."
But when I'm not thinking straight
I sometimes write unwisely
and rashly hit "send."
Only then, too late,

do I begin to wait.
Filled with dawning
apprehension and
the weight of regret,
I wait for the reply
or the phone call
or the stiff silence
of the loved one
whose trust
my late-night words
were betraying.
Yes, there is something
to be said
for not saying.
Especially in the middle of the night.

Intimate Mysteries

Green Mother

One of the potato vines is looking
unhappy, raggedy, sickly,
like it's under the weather in some way…
its little leaves are clasped
and pointing up,
like praying hands,
revealing shy purple undersides…
some of its branches look root-like,
brown and brittle at the tips…
a mystery condition the local
nurseryman has confidently
diagnosed as possibly
"too much water…
or not enough."

And because it is August,
because the big pots are so densely
threaded with hair-like roots,
because the weather we are under
includes winds that whip through
off the Bay and the ocean
at velocities worthy of wind-tunnels,
evaporating any moisture
in our soil and air and skin,
I decide to water,
to err on the side of water,
to give the vines a drink.

And I am standing beside
one of the potato vine pots,
holding the green garden hose,
letting the water run
until I can see it flow out
the bottom of the pot,
streaming in gleaming rivulets
onto the surrounding concrete,
when suddenly I feel
a tap on my shoulder.

And when I turn in response
to see who it is,
I find it is
the vine that has tapped me.
And what floods over me,
is the feeling "mother,"
a feeling so physical,
it is like the letting down
of my milk when I held
my baby at my breast,
like the primal response
when my baby
would cry out in the night,
and I would go to him.

"Mother,"
the vine,
my child,
has called me.
And while I am still
feeling the universe
re-order at the word,
the vine reaches out to me,
to touch me again,
caressing my cheek,
the way some babies do,
the way they stroke
a strand of your hair,
hang onto your finger,
or pat your breast so gently,
as you feed them
and they fall asleep in your arms.

Hello, my little vine.
What do you need?
I am smiling,
loving you,
hoping,
as I have once before,
that I will grow

in love and wisdom
as I tend a new life,
the new, greening life
that once was my child,
but now is you.
And maybe me.

My Pearl of Great Price

The book is still open in my mind.
I have been reading
a modern-day mystic's
thoughts on the spiritual life,
and I am beginning to understand
why during these last months
I have been strangely envious
of falling in love, of new lives,
and first-times of every kind.
I am beginning to understand
this aching sadness in me
for all the glad things that are over,
never to be new in me again.

Your new Love,
the mystics and ecstatic poets whisper,
is waiting for you.
They laugh,
"Your new Love has been
waiting for you all along,
waiting for you to step aside,
and vacate the place
you seem to have taken
at the center of the universe!"

"And what will you give," they ask,
"for the ecstasy of daily intimacy
with this, your Love Of All Loves…
what are you willing to give up
that you might be swept up
and given over completely
to the Most Precious Lover…
what will you give that you
might be an expression
of this Great Love
in the wearied world?"

"Oh, all!" I say, Everything!"

But in the next second
or hour or day,
I realize how much I lie.
For the staggering sacrifice required
for my pearl of great price
turns out to be,
quite simply and impossibly,
how I spend my time.

Seeing God for the First Time

The air is crisp and fresh
as laundry on the line.
I am five and walking
in a caterpillar
line of pre-schoolers,
all holding mittened hands
on this small-town street
on a morning in early spring.

My teacher points,
"Look!," she says, "A crocus!"
And I look and am so amazed,
joy-crazed,
to see--poking out of a
cracked, gray-dirty
end-of-winter snow cap
moored in a corner where
two sidewalks come together--
a tiny, purple-petaled egg bud.

I am just five.
This is my first crocus.
I am dazzled forever--
how glorious life is,
how much there is to know,
to see a thing so beautiful
rising from a crust of snow.

For John W.

Speaking In Tongues of Prayer

In a quiet room, two healing partners,
a man and a woman,
lean across the table
on which my young friend lies,
their love focused in their hands,
touching the body and life of my friend
who has so recently come through
the ordeal of radiation, chemo, and
two surgeries for brain cancer.
The healing partners ask my friend
by what name he prefers to address
the Divine; and he answers,
"Creator God."

One healing partner, I know--
an ordained minister with silver hair,
her voice and presence as comforting
as the soft velour sweater she wears.
You, her partner in this healing session,
are a slim man with a silver, close-cropped
beard, blue jeans, and an air of gentleness.
We have never met before,
and all I know about you is
what you told me
before we walked in:
that you feel called
to do this healing work.

Over the next half-hour both of you,
the healers, move quietly, slowly,
prayerfully touching specific points
along the length of my friend's body
in the ancient sacred healing ritual
of the laying on of hands.
The woman healing partner speaks
softly to my friend

from time to time.
And my friend lies quietly
receiving, receiving, and receiving
the love that is in these healing hands.
In the last moments of the healing,
you, the man I do not know,
begin to offer up a closing prayer,
using the name for the Divine
given by my friend:
Creator God.

"Create—Create—Create—or God,
We—we—we —th—th—thank—you…"
you stutter in a hushed and prayerful way.
I listen with my whole body.
I watch with my whole body.
I watch your lips feeling for the shape
of each word in the prayer.
Each word you say seems singular,
becoming cumulative,
like a string of prayer beads
strung along a silken cord.

Your mouth is beautiful on the words,
so genuine.
It is as if you are speaking,
or being spoken, in tongues,
the gentlest of tongues.
And when the prayer comes to its end,
you close with a stuttered "amen."
But the prayer lingers in the healing room.

Afterwards, as my friend takes time
to gather himself and his shoes,
I catch up with you outside.
I tell you how beautiful your prayer was.
You look at the ground, speaking carefully,
"I'm glad it came across…
in spite of…my stutter."

And I realize immediately
you don't understand.
"No, no," I say,
"Your prayer was beautiful
because of your stutter."
I try to tell you it carried
the power of the word,
so honest, so simple, so true.
It made me listen.
It made me feel Spirit
was listening, too.

I see you are startled, trying to take this in.
The others have caught up to us,
breaking our small bubble of private words.
And I must go…and in my going
I leave you standing there,
no doubt trying to reconcile a
life-long struggle with your stutter
with a possibility you may
never have considered before,
that your stutter might give your prayers
              power,
words repeating,
        repeating,
                repeating
                        for emphasis,
your tongue given over to a kind of
ecstatic diction and conviction,
compelling you to say again,
and yet again,
what we are seeking,
what we are feeling,
what we are exalting
in our intimate talk with God,
…who is here with us,
on our very tongues.

You pray like a poet.
You are a singer of Psalms.

Your words, your prayers, are healing.
And I thank—thank—thank our,
Create—Create—Create—or God
for calling your hands and
your stutter
to do God's healing work.

God's Eyes

It is the first day after a wild weekend
of autumn rainstorms—
trees threshing, eucalyptus rending
their bark garments into remnants
that fall in heaps at their feet,
roof shingles clapping like applause
for the bravura of this fearsome storm,
rain dripping in
through the bedroom ceiling,
rain water rushing in to form pools on the
garage floor and in the laundry room.

But today, the day after the storms,
all is quiet, polished with light,
fresh as dewy lettuce in a spring garden,
the sky swept blue,
the only telltale evidence
of nature's wild weekend:
storm drains so sated
they cannot drink another drop;
sodden litter everywhere,
marking the wake of the storm
like trampled trash and confetti
the morning after a big parade;
cars plowing wind rows
in the fallen leaves and twigs,
and at least a billion-trillion-million
coppery pine needles in the street.

I am out walking in the damp,
my unnamed yearning spiraling
up to consciousness again.
I'm walking and waking again
to this ever-deepening desire
to fall deeper into Love.
And I wonder
under that blue sky,
in the golden, autumnal light,

in the damp and leafy streets
how I might
practice the presence of God
in all the moments of my life,
how I might practice the presence of God
continually, like Brother Lawrence did
as he washed the dishes,
or peeled the potatoes,
or ate at the table,
or picked beans in the garden,
just a humble lay Brother
assigned to kitchen work,
practicing the presence of God
in every everyday moment of his life
in a monastery in the 1600's.

Just then, for but the blink of an instant,
my I vaporizes, goes to glow,
so close to my body's edges I am
only a vivified painting
on the walls and ceiling
of the Sistine Chapel
of my bodymindspirit.
I am I-not-I, only a film, color, a veil, a mist,
that lifts, hovering around openness.
And suddenly into that openness
pours the Holy One.
And this Mighty God, this Great Jehovah
is looking out
through my eyes…
and loving the beautiful, ravished,
burnished, damp, sweet world
and the autumn rainstorm street.

In the next instant, I pour, corporeal,
back into my bodymindspirit again,
stunned with a flashing realization,
knowing beyond any understanding,
that what I am is a God-holder,
that what you are is a God-holder, too.

That is what we are.

Whatever person, personality, body,
or petty or pious or impressive piece of
monkey-business I thought I was,
this I, I am, is amazingly
and only and always but
a vessel, a vase,
a satchel, a case,
a sachet, a human story
made up so miraculously,
to hold the Living God.

Windsocks

Two 4-foot Mylar windsocks,
sliced into long, lithe silver ribbons,
their entire lasered-holographic lengths
given over to the wind's abandon,
capering, twirling, spinning with the wind,
spangling, twinkling, flashing, flaring,
throwing off explosions
of tiny rainbow-fireworks
ignited by the sun.

Though I had hung the windsocks
on the deck several days before,
today I waken from a nap on the swing,
my eyes opening on this rainbow-dance
and see the windsocks, really see them,
for the first time.
I adore
the playful romp of light and shadow,
these exclamations of color
that spark and singe my heart.

And suddenly I am falling away from
this world of separateness and busyness,
falling into the arms of starry, spangled Love,
falling into shining, spinning Mystery,
a Mystery I am glimpsing here but dimly
in these dervish-dancing ribbons,
whirling me into the space of ecstasy…
astonishing me with the depth
of my desire to give myself
to the movement of God
as these windsocks give themselves
to the wind,
to give myself to every inhalation
and exhalation of the breath of Spirit,
to let go in absolute wonder and abandon
to being moved anywhere, in any way,
God is moved to move me.

So being tossed aloft,
rippled gently,
snared on twigs,
quieted, spun,
stilled in the moonlight
twirled in the noonday sun
were all the same,
this being moved by God
all I am or want or ask.

Available

Some sit cross-legged
in full- or half-lotus,
some dovin, some kneel,
some touch brows to the ground,
subduing their bodies,
counting their breaths,
speaking their mantras,
praying their beads,
reciting ancient prayers.

But what about me?
I know, I know, I know
I need a spiritual practice.
But words pour out of my mind
like floodwaters bristling with debris,
images come to consciousness
in endless kaleidoscopes of chaos,
my body kinks, seizes, throbs,
and pin-prickles in its
outrage at being ignored.
Which might be exactly
the place to begin
for some.
But apparently not for me.

But now some innate knowledge
seems to be breaking through,
leading me to quiet music,
drawing me down to sit cross-legged
on the green, flowered rug,
compelling me to wait,
my hands relaxed and open,
until I am being so still
with the music flowing down
over me like a lullaby of rain
that I begin to be aware of a gentle
pulsing in my hands,
begin to give myself over

so I am what wants to be,
allowing myself to be moved,
allowing myself to be spun
by something wholly Other.

…a most delicate pressure on my hand,
a whisper-soft push on my elbow,
almost imperceptible urgings
until I realize I am moving,
no, being moved,
being the movement,
my hands sweeping,
being swept,
my arms following like silken ribbons,
my head and torso
arcing and swaying,
moving and spinning,
drawn by the music
into the only-ness of now.

And when my mind goes wandering,
strays off into wondering,
I call myself back to stillness again.
And I wait again
to be set into motion,
just being there,
only being there
willing to be moved
at the whim of,
in the rhythm of,
the Other.
When the sweet impulse comes again,
and gradually my body becomes
the movement again,
I sigh with the relief
of letting my self go
and tumble into ecstasy.
I am a body filled with grace!
Moving…
being moved…

moving…
being moved…
so wholly and utterly
without effort
I can't tell moving
from being moved.
And I wonder:
What if in my whole life
I could be as available as this?
What if I could be this "yes,"
so that in every moment of my life
God could move me like this?

And God must be wondering what if, too.

For my sister, Molly

Getting the Message

God sent me an e-mail yesterday.
God used my sister's hand.
After all the times I've prayed,
"Here I am, Lord...send me
...where will You send me?
...when will You send me?
...why don't You send me?
...have You sent me?
...is this Your work?
...is what I'm doing enough?
...am I enough?"
at last and again
the Holy One replied.

God spoke through my sister's words,
saying this and so much more:
"You are a see-er,"
making me understand
that I understand,
that I do it by taking Life to me
and *living* into the best
and the worst of it,
spinning straw into gold
the hard way--
by being the straw--
spinning suffering into compassion,
singularity into communion,
communion into healing love.

Straw into gold...
It is enough.
Especially for one who is so clay-footed.

God sent me an e-mail yesterday.
God used my sister's hand.

For Richard

Teeter-Totter

Teeter-totter, bread and water…
I can't remember the final lines
of the playground rhyme,
but I do remember how,
depending on your mood or meanness,
you could use the teeter-totter
to jolt your partner
with bone-crunching "cherry-bumps,"
or strand them up high
with their feet dangling down,
or keep them perfectly in balance.

I have this friend of forty-some years
who likes to keep in touch
by forwarding news articles,
opinion pieces,
and the occasional joke.
Most of the people on his e-mail list are,
almost certainly, ultra-conservative.
But I'm not.

At first I felt some obligation to read
all of the material he was sending,
but the stuff always left me fuming.
So I decided on a new tack
and deleted everything he sent
without even opening it,
so only the titles offended me.

Still, there were those titles!
Exasperated, I finally e-mailed him
to tell him I was the wrong audience
for what he was sending,
that I was deleting most of it,
because I found it offensive.

His reaction was level and kind:
"Well, hey, Ann, send me some
convincing material from the liberals.
I'd enjoy reading and discussing it."
He told me he remembered living in
California while he was in college,
how he very nearly got persuaded
that "tolerance was a good thing."

Oh boy. Now I knew for sure,
not in a million years,
were he and I ever going
to convince each other
of anything.

This morning's e-mail
brought the latest installment.
I was outraged as soon as I saw
this title pop into the subject line:
Pedophilia: The Next Civil Right?
Sitting alone in my office,
I stomped my foot.
I blew my lips out in a
spitty raspberry of derision.
How could people actually believe
their liberal friends were so
beyond the pale as to support
or defend such horrific ideas?

I put on my coat and hat
and took my mad out for a walk.
Somewhere between here and there
and back again,
I started thinking about teeter-totters.
I was experiencing these e-mails
as nasty cherry bumps.
But I know this guy;
I know he isn't really trying
to rattle my innards or jar my teeth.
He's just doing

what he sees as his job:
speaking out to make
the world a better place
according to his own set of values.

So he leans his way, and I lean mine—
as happens on any question
where there are differing opinions.
But what I had not seen before
is that the one who leans this way
needs the one who leans that way.
Because the world needs both
of them to keep a perfect balance.

The Zero in the O of NO

Mirror, mirror on the wall,
now I see you are not a mirror at all.
I expected a glimpse of my own reflection,
but instead see that you are the O in NO
and that the O in NO is a zero
I can stick my head clean through.

But why stop with just my head?
Head, shoulders, hips, legs, and feet,
I climb through the zero in the O of NO
to find nothing on the other side,
nothing but unlimited light
and infinite spaciousness.

In the center of all that generousness.
in golden block letters NO, O, zero
hangs suspended from invisible strings,
from invisible hooks,
from invisible sky.

NO, O, zero how artful you are!
To know NO is to clear confusion away.
NO stands alone,
an object for worship,
or fruitful contemplation.
Or I could make of it a swing,
the O like an inner tube,
a circle fashioned of the inner,
a point where I balance,
pumping my legs for momentum,
moving through space and time,
from here to there,
then there to here again,
the zero of O of NO
never the final answer
to a question,
but a decision point
that swings both ways.

Life, Death &
In Between

Vines

Woven tightly together,
like a heavy rug of knotted-wool,
the bright green vines
with their fluttering fringes of tiny leaves
must have been crawling up that
freeway wall through season upon season
of rain and sun and traffic,
reaching out with their tiny tendril hands
ever wider and higher,
tender tendrils turning to
heavier, stronger stock,
all clinging to each other, climbing the rock.

Today, a huge section of the vines
has fallen away from the wall,
the weight of the vines' many years
finally becoming heavier than
their finite ability to cling.

And so the rug of vines rolls back on itself,
in a long, slow-motion, backward dive,
falling so far from the top of the wall
the rug's leading edge
comes to rest on the ground,
the vines' ropey, gray underbelly
fully exposed.
And I wonder if the entire mat of vines
will die like that.
And more,
if I will die like that, too.

My dear, wise, and well-loved husband,
you and I planted
the vines of our lives side-by-side
nearly forty years ago.
In our youth we were
slender, green, and tender,
but over the years

we have both grown
stronger, sturdier,
our separate shoots,
reaching out at intervals
to grab onto each other
as we pulled ourselves
up the wall of years,
twining around each other,
all our bright green tendrils
toughening,
tightening into iron knots,
as we each and separately
climbed the wall,
each rising up on the strength
of the other.

Now, as we approach our 60th birthdays,
I wonder how many seasons we have left.
And when one of our life-vines flat-lines
or loses its hold on the wall and falls,
what will happen to the other then?
We have been entwined
in each other's embrace for so long,
will we come down together,
like the woven rug of freeway vines?
Will we be able to stand alone in our age,
having stood together for this long?

I go outside to the trellis and search
for clues among the potato vines.
Here and there
a brown vine dangles,
leaves withered,
brittle and dead.
The green vines entwined with it
still hold the dead-dying vine
in their knotted embrace.
The ghost-vine may wither and thin
with time, becoming nearly weightless,
slipping the bonds of the greener vines,

dropping away to disappear.
But now while the dying vine
still carries weight,
what prevents it
from taking down
the whole verdant network
of those attached to it?
I push back the leaves and look.
The green vines are reaching out
for connections in every direction.
They clasp vines close to them here
and there
        and there
                and there,
criss-crossing one another to loop
their thready tendrils
over this vine
and that
        and that
                and that,
like the weaving of green threads
in a delicate piece of handmade tatting.
And it is then I notice there is an
unfailing source of stability and strength
for the vines that will live on...
They do not cling to each other alone.
They reach out and twine themselves
in and out and around the trellis itself.

You, my husband, my dearest vine,
my life-long climbing partner,
the one I have always held
closest in my living embrace,
no matter which of us falls away first,
the knots we have created between us
have grown as hard as iron
and that love, our love, will live on
as part of the texture of the fabric
of this green life.

And you--my son, my daughter-in-law,
my family and friends--
are my beloved companion vines,
those in whose embrace I know
I will be able to lean and rest
in hard seasons of wind or drought,
of floods or loss,
as you know I will hold you
and let you lean on me.

But it is you, O God,
who are the Creative Darkness
from which all our green shoots spring.
You who are the green Life flowing
in all our roots, and stems, and leaves.
You who are the Magnum Mysterium
to which we will all return
at the moment of our death.
You who are the Divine trellis,
the sturdy, branching bough of Life,
unshakable, ever present to us
in limitless points of intersections
giving us unlimited opportunities
to wrap ourselves, hold fast, and cling.

Humble Pie

It's Turkey Day,
and this year,
for the first time,
my son and daughter-in-law
have made plans to
celebrate it with friends.
And we're invited.

At our knock, the holiday door
swings wide with welcome.
I hug our kids and their
funderful friends,
bring in my pumpkin pie
and brownies with walnuts,
put my goodies on the festive table,
put my coat on the bed,
...and put my hands in my pockets,
feeling strangely unsure
what in the world to do next,
since it's not my kitchen,
and it's not my mulled cider,
and it's not my turkey,
and it's not my mashed potatoes,
and it's not my buffet,
and it's not my house.

I gamely ask the hostess,
"Anything I can do?"
but no, everything is tended to.
And all the young women are
so preternaturally competent.
And all of the young people
sparkle with such lively energy.
And I can see it's really true
all there is for me to do
is snack
and chat
and learn to be a guest.

I'm not in the kitchen this year
cooking up the celebration.
I'm in the dining room now,
feeling naked without my apron.

And I already sense
I will have much further
to go on future holidays—
traveling all the way
across the vast reaches
of the family dining room
to my future in the living room,
where I will one day
be spending the duration
of each holiday celebration,
seated in an especially
soporific, comfy chair.

And I will know
just how old I am,
just how long it's been
since I bid my kitchen and
my hostessing days goodbye
when my grand-daughter
arrives at my side,
holding out a plate,
saying,
"Look, Grandma,
I brought you
your pie."

The Eyes of Death Are Deep

I am here on the charity hospice unit
for the first time,
here to sing with two other women.
We find wooden chairs in the vestibule
and carry them in with us,
so we can sit near the patients
as we move from bedside to bedside.

I notice that above each spotless bed
a white index card
has been push-pinned to the wall
with the patient's first name
hand-lettered on it in red marking pen.
Our first songs are for Mary...
a tiny, aged lady
so clean and fragile,
curled on her side,
her eyes staring in the mid-distance,
her mouth slack,
teeth like a jack-o-lantern,
skin as wrinkled and transparent
as microwaved plastic wrap.

We sing three quiet songs for Mary,
our voices seeming to pour out in a
warm, liquid, honeyed balm of love.
Mary briefly interrupts her stare
--she blinks once--
but that is all.
Like most of the others in these beds
and at the end of their days
or in a coma's pseudo-sleep,
Mary can no longer speak.

After we sing, we touch Mary's
motionless hand, say our goodbyes,
then move on from bed to bed
around the room,

still carrying our chairs,
sitting to sing for each person,
each one whose name we know now
by the writing on the wall.

When we reach the final bed,
the first bed on the unit,
we find a young man propped on pillows,
so young he seems incongruous
in this sanctuary for the frail elderly.
Brandon, the red letters
on his index card read.
Brandon coughs and coughs,
each cough causing him to slosh the coffee
he is drinking from a paper cup.
His ravaged body is covered only
by a discreetly-placed swath of sheet.
I can see immediately that
Brandon was once a beautiful man--
before his flesh and health were
eaten away by AIDS.
And Brandon is still beautiful now,
even with his gauntness and affliction,
his beard neatly trimmed,
his nipple ring a kind of giddy, daring,
giggling counterpoint in a place and
circumstance as serious as death.

Like so many of the others here,
Brandon does not speak,
but as we sing for him,
Brandon looks at us.
And when he does,
his eyes enter my eyes and pierce down
to something like the very
I-AMness of my being.
His eyes do not plead for mercy
or hold a single flicker of self-pity.
In truth, they are disconcerting,
almost merciless in the depth

they go within me.
And I wonder:

Just exactly who is looking at me here?
For it is a great dispassionate Power I see,
all-knowing, unending, all-embracing,
unflinching, deeper-darker than the grave.
And I wonder:
Am I looking at the eyes of God,
the in-dwelling Eternal Spirit looking out
in the in-between time just before
this robe of incarnation drops away?

Watchers

*Once upon a time
we held the center stage of Life;
we were in the spotlight,
that blindingly special, graced place
where people fall in love,
where babies are born,
where homes are made,
where careers are launched,
where children are raised.
But what happens when
our once upon a time
becomes a long time ago?*

Ed stoops over to slap dirt off his jeans.
He's been out here at the home place,
weeding a little, sitting a little, puttering.
Marian doesn't like to ride along anymore.
She gets too antsy to ever be a putterer.
She likes to keep busy and get things done
so she can cross them off her list.
But the neighbors who rent the fields don't care,
and his grand-daughter who's renting
the old farmhouse doesn't mind,
so Ed comes out to the farm
and just putters.
Ed understands Marian would like
to sell the farm now that they own
the little house in town.
And Marian understands Ed's not ready.
Ed pours a cup of coffee
from his Thermos,
sips his coffee slowly.
And Ed watches...

...watches the sun shining through the maple
leaves overhead, how it makes the leaves look
like they're made of red and gold cellophane

…watches how the honeysuckle vines are
clutching the edge of the garage roof, ready to
hoist themselves up and grow wild
…watches a bird light on the gate up by the barn
and recalls in a flash of memory the day
that skittish gelding was tied to the gate,
got startled by something, took off,
and ripped the gate off the fence post,
dragging the gate behind him,
so panicked by the gate chasing him,
he was nearly impossible to catch and untie.
Ed breathes in the scent of sun-warmed grass,
listens to the creak of the rusty weathervane
on the barn roof, lets his memories of life here
fill him up.
And Ed is smiling.

One day we look around and wonder,
where is the spotlight now?
Not on us. Not often anymore.
Life has been moving us,
gently nudging us,
toward the wings,
giving us support roles
and character parts…
the friend, the uncle, the grandmother.
We're becoming ourselves so much
we've started to turn into characters.

Vihalia sits on her front porch, rocking,
her shoelaces untied to give her feet
some breathing room.
Her glass of lemonade
sweats a glistening circle
on the chipped white table beside her.
Now and then she waves an ancient fan printed
with a local funeral parlor's name
to make a little breeze on her face and neck.
Vihalia is humming her favorite hymn,
"The Lord Laid His Hand on Me,"

in an unhurried rhythm.
Her feet are pumping,
the chair is rocking,
moving in the same
unhurried rhythm as the hymn.
Even with her shoes on,
she can feel how satiny smooth
the floor has become from all the afternoons
she's rocked on the porch just like this.
And Vihalia watches...

...watches Princess, her dainty-footed dowager
cat, tiptoe along the entire length of the white
porch railing
...watches the way the green-tiered spires of
pink hollyhocks sway in the wake of Princess'
passing
...watches two little boys with bare feet, sitting
on a stoop across the street, sucking and licking
on Popsicles and laughing
...watches the storm clouds boiling in her
direction, takes in the first drop of rain,
the low rumbling thunder, cracks of lightning,
the smell of dust being settled in the street,
in the driveway, and flower bed,
and the sound of rain on the porch roof.
Vihalia tips her head back, her eyes closed.
And Vihalia is smiling.

Then the time comes when we don't
even have a place in the wings anymore.
We're older and look where that puts us
now in the great theater of Life...
in the audience,
but in the front row,
maybe the best seats,
so we're cheering, applauding,
laughing, crying,
still close enough to feel a part of the show,
still close enough to see the stars sweat

and feel the spit fly.

Peter isn't able to get out to walk around
the neighborhood the way he used to.
This morning he's feeling so raggedy,
he's still in his robe and pajamas at 10:30.
But he's content to be in his recliner chair,
right where he asked his grandson to move it:
in front of the picture window.
He jokes he's got a season pass
for the outdoor theater now.
He keeps his binoculars right beside him.
And Peter watches…

…watches the birds flipping rhinestones
of water from the birdbath, flying to the feeders
and knocking down about twice as much seed
as they eat
…watches the squirrels running to skitter up the
trunks of the pine trees, leaping from bough to
bough like circus daredevils wearing costumes
with bottle-brush tails.
…watches one black squirrel warily making its
way--scurry-scurry-stop, scurry-scurry-stop--
right up to the window in front of him,
snatching sunflower seeds strewn on the sill
outside, looking inside directly at Peter for
several seconds.
And Peter is smiling.

And finally one day,
we find ourselves
in the balcony
of the theater of Life.
We wouldn't have thought
it would be like this:
what a view, what a privilege,
such perspective.
From up here we can watch the stage,
and the audience at the same time.

*From up here we can catch nuances
that might make or break the play,
get inspirations about what is needed next,
anticipate entrances and exits,
take in the big picture
and what it takes to make
the play make sense.*

Vera was just pronounced queen-for-a-day,
and her gold plastic crown with plastic jewels
made it official. Today is her 80th birthday,
and this must be the best surprise party ever!
Her grandson's house is crammed with in-laws
and outlaws, kids and grandkids, and great-
grandkids. As the queen and birthday-girl, she
got to go to the head of the line to fill her plate
from a pot-luck buffet laden with special dishes.
She ate too much, but the food was so good
she wanted to clean her plate with a spatula.
Now she's sitting contentedly on the couch
with a plate of birthday cake in her lap.
And Vera watches…

…watches four great-grandsons intent on their
video game, their hands, their perfect hands, so
quick on the joysticks
…watches her sweet great-grand-daughter enter
the room, and motions her to come closer,
come closer--until the girl is close enough to be
snuggled up in a one-arm, great-grandma-
holding-cake embrace
…watches and laughs as another great-grand
tries to toddle around with both legs thrust into
one leg of his snap-seam pants
…watches her three grown children,
so different,
so alike,
so all in cahoots today
as they act out hilarious family stories about her,
and the whole house rocks with laughter.

Imagine.
All three of her kids joking, plotting,
laughing, and talking together,
all the rancor of some difficult years,
now past,
gone,
and forgiven.
And from where she sits, Vera sees it all,
and has some trouble swallowing around
the lump of gratitude, answered prayer,
and blessing in her throat.
And Vera is smiling.

Life longs for our love,
needs for us to notice it
in all its wonders, aches,
profusions, and glories.
May it be that
as we grow older,
we may also grow
in our willingness
to become watchers,
abandoning our busy-ness
to give fully to Life
our complete attention,
appreciating Life with
our whole hearts
our whole minds,
our whole spirits,
and all our senses.
When we do,
Life watches us watch…

And Life is smiling.

For Mary Ann

Yes-Ma'm

You've heard of a Yes-Man,
Well, Mary Ann is a Yes-M'am,
and that's an entirely, totally
and altogether different thing.
What Mary Ann seems so
miraculously able to say yes to
is Life.

She said yes to destiny and history
when she enlisted
as a WAVE and became a
medic in World War II.

She said yes to her complexities
when she entered college to study
occupational therapy and art…
improbably taking courses
in accounting, too,
because she had to drive
to school anyway and, well,
accounting looked interesting.

She said yes when only one child
came to bless her marriage and her life.
And she said yes the day
she and her husband
had to pace and pace and pace
up and down the street
beside their only child,
a young man then,
trying to talk him
          down ,
trying to talk him down
and into the hospital
where he was diagnosed
with schizophrenia…

a drama and a diagnosis
they still deal with every day,
still, after all these years,
living together in the same house.

I've often wondered, even marveled
at what allows Mary Ann
to stay so big-hearted,
so able to keep saying yes to
what is sometimes a difficult life,
without growing hardened ,
without withdrawing into bitterness,
without pretending things are
any way but what they are.
And recently I think I got it,
what may be at the center
of Mary Ann's secret salvation,
the Y and E and S
of her yes.

When too much is being asked...
when pain, helplessness, grief or anger
start to overwhelm her...
when she is parched and drained,
she goes to the well
of her creativity,
letting down her well-worn,
mossy, wooden bucket,
drawing up from the deep,
quenching drafts of inspiration
she pours out as art,
manifesting strength, beauty,
peace, order, or ordered chaos
in a paper-on-glass-plate collage,
or an in-genius handmade book
shaped like a circus tent,
or a hand-painted silk scarf
water-marked by rock salt,
or a necklace of Venetian beads or bones
or silver or chunks of sun-dried potato,

or a one-of-a-kind bookmark worked
from chunky beads and twisted wire,
or a burn-carved and polished gourd,
or yet another, other
more magical, expressive
extraordinary thing.

Mary Ann's heart
and bucket
delve deep,
bring forth,
pour out
beauty, healing
and acceptance
drawn up from the
infinite creative place
where God lives.

For Dulcie, always and ever my friend

Birthing Her Mother

"Hello, you," my friend says
when I chance to reach her
on her cell phone somewhere
between home and the hospital.
I hear her calm and her strength,
though her voice has obviously
been grated and shredded
on the rough grief-tool of crying.

My friend's mother is 90.
After weeks of failing and falling,
hitting her head,
blackening her eye,
purpling her face,
her mother has now suffered
two strokes in rapid succession.
Cruel harbingers of death,
the strokes are stealing away
her mother's humanity
one muscle, one synapse, one nerve,
one body function at a time,
leaving her mother's left side paralyzed;
her tongue, lips, mouth and throat
unable to eat, or swallow, or speak.
And yet with all that is lost
I can tell my friend still
senses love and recognition
in her mother's eyes.
.
On the phone, my friend hastily
tells me before she has to hang up,
"We're trying to find someone
to come in to provide 24-hour care,
and we're lining up Hospice
so we can bring Mom home to die
in her own home in her own bed."

And though this is a pronouncement
of the grim truth that there is no hope,
I sense the presence of hope
surrounding my friend like a nimbus,
lifting her up in this vision
of how she wants things
to be for her mother
in her mother's last hours or days.

That was yesterday.
This morning I find an e-mail
from my friend
written sometime during the night.
Trying to untangle the knot
of wiry, unyielding rational thoughts
and deep and tightly-wound feelings,
she wrote of her anguish
over the decisions she must now make
about feeding tubes, hydration,
oxygen, and medications,
knowing her mother
has been firm
about not wanting
any heroic measures,
feeling selfish for wanting
to keep her mother here with her--
even if only for a little while longer.

I read my friend's words,
my chest tight with her anguish.
But then in my mind and my heart
I find myself moving with her
through these wrenching decisions,
remembering how my
friend's voice sounded
when she spoke of bringing
her mother home to die
in her own bed.
I picture her mother there,
at home, in her own bed...

clean sheets and soft blankets
tucked around her…
the light in the room soft as the blankets…
the quiet comfort of familiar things,
and my friend holding her mother
in her arms, loving her,
whispering her gratitude and blessings,
birthing her mother into death
just as her mother once
birthed her into life.

Not Too Distressed

At 60 and 62, we finally outgrew
the disguised-plywood platform bed
on which our mattress has rested
for more than thirty years,
all the years since the mattress
replaced our air-frame waterbed.
Hari krishna, krishna, krishna.

Our new bedroom furniture
arrived two weeks ago
after a six-month wait,
looking mighty fine
and, exactly as ordered,
slightly distressed--
only slightly distressed
because any more distressed
would have distressed
the new-should-look-new
engineer with whom
I share all my beds.

I admit I have a love affair
with beauty of any and every kind,
and this new furniture kisses my eyes.
Each time I catch a glimpse of it
I sigh with pleasure over the airy
and arched cane foot- and headboards,
the lovely little bedside dressers,
the antiqued, creamy, painted wood,
every curve and carve and turning of it.

Two nights ago before I went to sleep
I laid my glasses down on the dresser top,
and they made that little clicking,
coming-to-rest noise glasses do,
glass and metal ticking against wood.
As I turned out the light I thought...

Someday when we're gone
our son will have to come
to empty the house.
Will he notice on my dresser top
the little worn place
where I've laid my glasses
down each night of all
my remaining
coming and going years?

I find I'm not as distressed
as I once was to think upon
all this slowly wearing down,
all this marring and slackening,
all this fading and spotting and pocking
of stair steps and shoes and books,
of chairs and tabletops and bodies.
The Japanese have a word for it;
they call it Wabisabi—
a veneration and respect
for the beauty
of the impermanent,
of the imperfect,
of what has been worn by life,
the unique history testified to
by all the scars and imperfections
that tell and are our story.

Call in the Crows

May it not be so...
But if death comes for
my husband, my love, first,
I pray a flock of giant crows
will be quick to come to me.

I pray the crows will rush in like a fierce wind,
beating the air in their fury,
landing in the trees, on the rooftop,
on the porch,
beside me,
stalking in my darkened door,
entering the house without knocking.

I pray the crows will come to me
with all their black wings
spread like capes,
their ragged feathers
dragging the ground
like tattered mourning clothes.

I pray the dark birds will encircle me,
call out of me my crow-self,
urging me to
caw,
scold,
scream,
screech,

spurring me to
thrust out my neck,
crow-like,
strain forward,
crow-like,
making the cacophonous,
outraged sounds
spew out,
my beaky mouth,

my only tool or weapon
to give expression to my grief.

May it not be so...
But if death comes for
my husband, my dearest friend, first,
I pray that all the widows,
all the childless mothers,
all my tribal sisters of the world,
will come to me in spirit,
drawn by the primordial sound of
another human's death-watch weeping.

I pray my sisters will persuade me
to give my body to my grief,
so I pound the ground,
tear my clothes,
throw dust on my head,
clasp my arms around myself
and rock my empty frame.

I pray they will be my midwives,
calling out of me
all my wailing grief,
urging me to pant with the pain,
helping me to bring to birth
the fullness of my sorrow.

I pray my sisters will draw me down
to fall on my knees among them,
all of us leaning into one another,
our arms locked around each other,
our tongues untied,
ululating together
in that piercing,
harrowing vocalization
of unbearable sorrow…
the sorrow
we forget
we risk

at every moment
we love
with all our heart and soul
someone
so fatally mortal.

May it not be so...
But if death comes for
the other half of my heart first,
I will call in the crows.
I will call in my tribal sisters.
But I warn all others:
If my loving man
dies before me,
don't come near me
if emotionality unnerves you.

For I will not take his death well.
 ...I will grieve down the house.

I will not pull myself together.
 ...I will fall apart in a thousand
 scrambled, jig-saw pieces.

I will not bear up with quiet courage.
 ...I will make loud, unseemly scenes
 and embarrass the family.

I will not wanly dab my eyes with Kleenex.
 ...I will soak the songbooks and
 drown the carpets with my tears.

And I will not find comfort in any of your trite-
and-true or tried-and-true condolences.
 ...I will choke on your words if you try to
 talk to me then of God's plan or how my
 love is in a better place. Wait.

If death comes for this man I love first,
I will not exhibit

any
sugar-coated, over-rated, funereal virtues.
  …I will be inconsolable.
  …I will scorch the pews with my passion.
  …I will weep over what is left of his body:
    just a shoeboxful of ashes.
  …I will believe I can't go on without him.

And there will be nothing anyone can do.
So let me go to live
among the crows
for a time.
The crows will let me be.
They will let me tell all my stories
about this prince of a man
and the life we had together,
let me tell the same stories
over and over,
as many times as I need to,
until I don't need to tell them anymore,
until finally I discover the Love
I thought I'd lost,
still alive,
in the deepest center of my Self,

and can come back into the world
to love it all again
  …for both of us.

We Can See It from Here

I've heard other people—in the
generation before us--say it.
And I always drop a stitch
in the fabric of the conversation
when they speak the words
so matter-of-factly,
when the fact of the matter
seems so extraordinary to me.
Then last night my husband
remarked that even
though our newer car
is still reasonably shiny
and powered by high-test horses,
it's actually eleven years old…
and next year we may need
to take on car payments again
to get a newer model coming off lease.
Something in my head did
a little involuntary calculation.
"Wow," I said, "Just think, if
we keep that car for eleven years,
you'd be 74 years old when
we traded it in for another car."
We turned to each other with
the same thought and phrase
on our tongues, practically
speaking the words in unison:
And that will probably be
the last car we'll ever buy.
Just what all those older others
have said: our last car.
What a shock: this is us.
We can see
the end of the road
from here.

For my brother, Frank Eugene Brownson,
November 18, 1952--March 15, 2004
Written for Frank's memorial service.

What You Left

You left your lunch bucket
sitting on the kitchen counter,
home too early to be empty,
your coffee cup on top.

You left a row of pill bottles
containing the lying medicines
that never fully cut the pain
in your legs, your knees,
your back, your elbows
or your heart.

You left your fire-pit in the backyard,
only ashes under the snow now,
but your gathering-in place
in other seasons of your life,
lawn chairs to sit in,
a campfire of communion
that somehow eased both
your inner and outer hurts.

You left your hunting clothes,
your lantern, your turkey feathers,
a deer skull, and a rack of antlers.
You left your crossbow and rifles
exactly where you last laid them,
not knowing you would never
take them up to aim or shoot again.

You left your work boots untied,
their laces dangling down,
your jeans in the closet,
your vest, your flannel shirts,
and not one thing fancier than

the way you saw yourself.

You left your deer stand,
your patient waiting-places,
your fishing haunts,
your secret mushroom-hunting caches,
and the woods and creeks
that were your mending places,
your counselors, your churches.

You left all these things, the seen,
but of the unseen
you have left us so much more.
You are leaving us with memories…

…memories of a tiny baby boy
born prematurely, your legs like hot dogs,
your fingers like needles…

…memories of a snapshot taken the following
summer showing someone helping you stand
up in a make-shift wading pool—biggie boy!—
and you're a baby sumo wrestler…

…memories of a sweet baby so loved
by family that one Sunday in church
your brother whispered to your mother,
"Mama, hold the baby up,
so everyone can see him."…

…memories of mama picking you up out of the
bathtub, wrapping a towel round and round
you, singing "Whirl my turban,
man alive, here comes Mr. 5 by 5"

…memories of that beat-up duffle bag
filled with who-knew-what you hauled
around for months on end until the
fateful day both you and the bag
fell into the stink of the Shawm-poo…

...memories of all the nicknames
you endured, the ones we, your siblings,
were so mercilessly good at inventing:
Horb,
Crazy Otto,
Pal
Knarf
(when you went to school
and quite naturally, left-handedly
spelled your name backwards)
and strangest of all, for a short time,
Puer,
because you had a solo in a pageant
and made the mistake of singing
in front of us: Puer natus est.
Puer meaning boy in Latin.
And later, of course, you became
Man or Manly.
How did you tolerate all our attention?

Beyond memories,
you are leaving with us the
blessed, brutal wisdom that comes
from enduring life's hardest lessons.
From our love for you,
from being kin or friend to you...

...we have learned what it is to
hang-in, stand by, stay in loving
relationship with someone
who is living angry, hard, and fast,
sometimes hurting others,
more often, hurting himself...

...we have learned to abide with
what we do not fully understand,
accept that we cannot change another,
that we cannot control another,
that we can only love another
until the time for change has come...

...we have learned what it is like to live
in the continual midnight of depression
without flashlight or lantern,
what it is to have the life taken
out of you, though you yet live,
to long for something better
but seeing no way out to find it...

...we have learned, too, of the release
that is born of forgiveness,
letting go of yesterdays,
of the things you couldn't
or wouldn't talk about,
finding that in our forgiving
we heal not only the person
we forgive,
but we also heal ourselves.

You are leaving a little bit of yourself
with so many of us, Frank....

...all of the outdoor lore you've been
collecting in fields and forests,
ponds and streams for all these years
resides in your sons, your wife and anyone
whoever talked with you at length.
My own suburban brain is indelibly
imprinted with the wonderment I felt
the day you told me some small birds
migrate by hitch-hiking
on larger birds' backs.
I see a bird and think of that,
and you are with me...

...your love of sports, your grasp of
baseball and football strategies and skills
you have handed off to all the kids
you ever helped to coach.
Because of you, these kids

know how to throw a pass or catch one,
how to block, and kick, and tackle,
how to swing a bat or field a baseball,
how to play every game to win
and keep your cool even if you lose.
Every time these kids play a game,
even when they coach their own kids,
you will be there, Frank, playing ball again.

...the mere fact that you got out of bed
and stood up in that sack of rasping joints,
busted knees, wrecked vertebrae,
flaming tendons and darkling deeps
that was your mind and body...
the mere fact that you got yourself
to work, however far away,
to wire a hospital, a field house,
or a steel mill in any kind of weather
was a testament to your diligence.
The guys you worked with had to know
you'd do what you said you'd do.
That's *showing* how it's done,
not telling.
You showed us all how it is done.
And your diligence goes with us.

...you are here and will be here,
in your children and your grandchildren.
You show up as curly hair or brown eyes,
or a love of sports or the natural world,
or a born-to-be-wild, Harley-riding streak,
or vulnerability tucked away under a rock,
or a kind of quiet, pensive inwardness.
The joy your children and grandchildren
brought you, the pride you had in them,
the hard times you struggled through
and mended together have shaped them
and all whose lives their lives will touch.
You are still here, Frank,
within each one of them,

still living in their loving.

...And most of all, you are here with Sherry,
who loved you ever since she was a girl,
and finally had you as her husband,
though she probably had no idea
just what all that was going to mean.
Of all who stood by you,
Sherry has been the most steadfast,
the closest to your pain,
the closest to your depression,
the closest to your love.
You will go on in Sherry
in the muscles of inward strength
she has been building all these years
just living with you.
You will be here watching Frankie's
games through Sherry's eyes.
You will be here to dandle the
grandbabies and great-grandbabies
on Sherry's knee.
You will be here as an ache
in Sherry's heart,
then like a well-loved, remembered song,
then as some of the most beloved chapters
in the book of her life.

...And all the woods and ponds and
streams remain your sanctuary, Frank.
For even trees and leaves and loamy earth,
and all the leaping, furry, shining,
flying, creeping, crawling creatures
need to be noticed and loved
and no one did that better than you.

My brother, you have left your body
behind in both seen and unseen ways.
You have asked that some of your ashes
be scattered in the woods, and in the creek
so, as you said, you can "flow on forever."

And so it shall be.
But even now, already, dear brother,
you are scattered here among us.
Through your family and your friends
all you have loved and all who loved you,
you are already flowing on forever.

For my brother, Frank

The Last Time

I remember grinning and nodding,
recognizing the feeling
the comedian was describing,
how when you're eating cookies
without really paying attention,
you may stick your hand
in the bag, bowl or box
and discover you already ate
the last cookie…
but you didn't know it,
so you didn't savor it like
the *last* cookie,
didn't calibrate your desire
and appreciation
to the fact that
the last cookie you ate
was the *last*.

Now I remember the cookies
and think of my brother.
Frank died two weeks ago.
The last time I saw him was last fall
when I visited my family in Ohio.
But I didn't know then
it would be the last time
I saw Frank.

On that trip I felt a curious desire
to step into Frank's life with him,
so I went to watch his team
of eleven-year-old boys play football,
to watch my brother be their coach.
And I asked Frank to take me
to the woods with him,
because the woods and fishing,
deer and turkey hunting

were so central to Frank's life.

"Aaah, you don't want to do that,"
he said to his long-gone-to-California,
city-fied sister,
half-way grinning behind his beard
in that half-secret way of his.
"No, really, I do," I said.
"You don't have any boots," he said.
"I could borrow some," I said.
But he grinned it off, not believing.
And I let the moment pass.
And now I will never be able
to go to the woods
with Frank.

The thing is,
I can never know when
the song I'm singing,
the embrace I'm wrapped in,
the words I'm speaking,
the walk I'm taking,
the kiss I'm giving,
the poem I'm writing,
the moment I'm living
might be my last.
So wake me!
Make me attend!
Let me revel in all my senses,
all my beloveds, all my living…
so I do not gobble up my days
like a bag of cheap cookies,
wolfing down a lifetime
of cookie-moments,
without taking time to taste them.
Let me live
every moment
as if this
cookie-moment
might be my last.

For my brother, Frank

The Golden Cord

We always *assumed*
the golden cord of family ties,
just *assumed* it was there
binding us together,
connecting us
like an intricate web of strings
wrapped 'round the fingers
of a child's hands
in a game of Cat's Cradle.
We *assumed* the golden cord
so well we largely ignored it,
tending to face outward
from the family circle,
focused on our separate lives…
until
so impossibly,
so suddenly,
so catastrophically,
our brother/husband/father/son died.
Wrapped 'round in the golden cord
we had only *assumed*,
Frank fell away from the world,
away from the circle of our family…
cinching the cord around us as he went,
his absence drawing us together,
pulling us tight,
making us realize
life is short,
but love is long.
If only we had known this
before
we lost Frank.

Charade

I dream I am in a gymnasium,
part of the audience
for something--
a class,
a workshop,
a game show—
exactly what,
I do not know.
We are seated in orderly fashion,
in rows and rows of chairs
lined up in a perfect square,
and my chair is near the
outside towards the front.

Our host or leader is talking,
but I am not listening,
because what is going on here
has nothing to do with me.
But I hear him
when he says,
"Let us begin."
And I watch
as four figures appear,
all dressed in long black robes
with cavernous hoods,
only darkness
where their faces should be.

The hooded figures move
silently through the audience,
each seeking a different person.
When all four have found
the people they've been looking for,
they each hold forth a white card
which the chosen ones
have no choice
but to choose.
And on each white card is printed,

in black letters, a single word,
a word specific to the person
to whom it has been given.

While the hooded figures search,
I am still not paying attention,
still thinking this has
nothing to do with me,
when one of the hooded figures
stops square in front of my chair
and hands me a card.
And I must take it.
And the card says: Rich

I am plunged into confusion.
But I wasn't listening, I object.
I don't know what I'm supposed to do.
This has nothing to do with me.
But we four who have been singled out,
stand up and begin to move
toward the front of the group
in a procession of
inexorable progression.

Even as I'm moving to the front,
I continue my objections,
This has nothing to do with me.
I don't even know how to play this game.
But no one explains,
so I am left to guess from
the actions of others
and my own instincts
the rules of the game
and how they might apply to me.

All four of us arrive at the front.
Time has run out.
Obviously, this does
have something to do with me.
I must act.

Yes, I will act out my word,
and try to get the audience
to say the word aloud: "Rich."

I begin…
and end
the dream
in a charade.
Outside the dream,
I awake from the charade
to the inescapable actuality
of my own aging.

It pokes me like a sharp stick.
I can feel it
pushing me toward the fore,
toward the front line
of the generations,
where death walks about
and singles us out,
where death
has everything to do with us,
everything to do with me.

I don't want to remember.
I want to continue my forgetting,
but I have no armor against
dreams or ordinary moments
…when death and life
swoop up in me together,
like a flight of cave-dwelling bats,
a flock of church-going swallows,
…when all in an instant,
as I'm lying on my back on my swing,
looking up into a poplar tree,
I feel a flood of love for that tree,
for all its chartreuse extravagance
of fluttering fans,
for all the splendor of its
luminosity and shadows.

And my heart leaps up
like it wants to wrap itself
up in the tree,
like it wants to fix
this beautiful, ordinary thing
in my memory…
in case I never
get to see it again.
I want to carry that poplar tree
with me when I go.
I feel the time coming now,
perhaps far off,
perhaps not,
when I will, in reality, receive
the card that ends the game.

But I can begin to imagine
now
the once-shocking possibility
that my body, my bones and spirit
will someday be so worn and weary,
I will want to,
long to,
leave behind
the weight of body and ego-self
and return
to the weightless darkness
of the Other Side,
to the dichotomous Healing Light,
to the Ground of My Own Being,
to the Source of This Wondrous All.
And I realize I want to
practice
my dying then,
to die just a little bit,
bit by bit learning to make
my peace with death
by laying my body
down on the earth
in a little hollowed place

filled with fallen leaves.

The word I was given for this Life,
the word with which I will leave it is: Rich.
So while I am still here,
let me live Rich,
giving my heart every chance
to wrap itself in
…chartreuse poplar leaves,
…magenta-throated star-gazer lilies,
…the black cat's green eyes
peering at me through the fence,
…the softness of my own belly,
…telling stories at the table,
…laughing with my husband
in the night,
…singing with such joy
it feels like Spirit is geysering
out the top of my head
in a fountain of light.

Let me give my heart every chance
to wrap itself
round and round and round
in the velvet Richness of Life,
the Richness of every simple thing,
every lovely simple thing,
…lovely chocolate pudding,
…lovely cup of tea,
…lovely reading in bed,
…lovely freshening of raindrops,
…lovely rhythms for feet and hips,
…lovely silence of a summer night,
…lovely autumnal walks,
…lovely winter naps,
…lovely cooling fog,
…lovely warm socks,
…lovely passionate disagreements,
…lovely forgiveness,
…lovely blessings,

...lovely life.

The youthful charade of
immortality is over.
I am dying.
How much more reason,
then,
to live...
how much more reason
to live
Rich.

Ann Keiffer loves beauty, color, words, wordplay, wit, laughter, light and shadow, creativity, people in all their complexities, the Divine Mystery wherever we may seek and find it, and times for every purpose under heaven. Ann is ordained as an Interfaith Minister of the Arts. She and her husband Larry live in San Mateo, California. Ann is also author of a non-fiction account of her own experience with deep depression, *Gift of the Dark Angel: A Woman's Journey through Depression Toward Wholeness*, as well as another book of poems, *Somebody's Life*. Ann and her son John Keiffer are creators of a traveling exhibit of poetry and black-and-white art photographs focused on the transforming possibility of depression.

www.ingramcontent.com/pod-product-compliance
Lightning Source LLC
Chambersburg PA
CBHW031955080426

42735CB00007B/404